INTRODUCTION TO CHEMISTRY

NOTES

COLES EDITORIAL BOARD

Bound to stay open

Publisher's Note

Otabind (Ota-bind). This book has been bound using the patented Otabind process. You can open this book at any page, gently run your finger down the spine, and the pages will lie flat.

ABOUT COLES NOTES

COLES NOTES have been an indispensible aid to students on five continents since 1948.

COLES NOTES are available for a wide range of individual literary works. Clear, concise explanations and insights are provided along with interesting interpretations and evaluations.

Proper use of COLES NOTES will allow the student to pay greater attention to lectures and spend less time taking notes. This will result in a broader understanding of the work being studied and will free the student for increased participation in discussions.

COLES NOTES are an invaluable aid for review and exam preparation as well as an invitation to explore different interpretive paths.

COLES NOTES are written by experts in their fields. It should be noted that any literary judgement expressed herein is just that – the judgement of one school of thought. Interpretations that diverge from, or totally disagree with any criticism may be equally valid.

COLES NOTES are designed to supplement the text and are not intended as a substitute for reading the text itself. Use of the NOTES will serve not only to clarify the work being studied, but should enhance the readers enjoyment of the topic.

ISBN 0-7740-3409-2

© COPYRIGHT 2004 AND PUBLISHED BY
COLES PUBLISHING COMPANY
TORONTO - CANADA
PRINTED IN CANADA

Manufactured by Webcom Limited
Cover finish: Webcom's Exclusive **DURACOAT**

CONTENTS

UNIT I — INTRODUCTION TO CHEMISTRY AS AN EXPERIMENTAL SCIENCE 5

UNIT II — ATOMIC STRUCTURE 10

UNIT III — THE STRUCTURE OF AGGREGATES OF ATOMS......................... 17

UNIT IV — STATES OF MATTER 22

UNIT V — VALENCE, FORMULAS, NOMENCLATURE AND EQUATIONS.................... 35

UNIT VI — OXYGEN 40

UNIT VII — HYDROGEN 47

UNIT VIII — ATOMIC WEIGHTS, MOLECULAR WEIGHTS AND MOLES 52

UNIT IX — CALCULATIONS FROM EQUATIONS 62

UNIT X — WATER AND SOLUTIONS 64

UNIT XI — IONS IN AQUEOUS SOLUTION 71

UNIT XII — THE ALKALINE EARTH ELEMENTS (GROUP 2) 81

UNIT XIII — THE HALOGEN ELEMENTS (GROUP 7) 88

UNIT XIV — THE PERIODIC CLASSIFICATION 100

UNIT I: INTRODUCTION TO CHEMISTRY AS AN EXPERIMENTAL SCIENCE

1. CHEMISTRY AS A SCIENCE

Chemistry deals with the substances of which the universe is composed and the changes they undergo. Other sciences and industries depend to a great extent upon chemistry — for example:

(i) **Medicine** — production and testing of antiseptics, anesthetics, drugs, etc.

(ii) **Food** — preparation, digestion, and assimilation are chemical processes.

(iii) **Clothing** — manufacture of synthetic fibres, dyes, etc.

(iv) **Cosmetics** — manufacture of soaps, toothpaste, etc.

(v) **Transportation** — manufacture of metals, fuels, lubricants.

Mathematics, physics and chemistry are considered to be the three basic sciences but these themselves are closely related — for example:

(i) it is impossible to separate the studies of physical and chemical properties of substances.

(ii) a knowledge of mathematics is necessary to the chemist in order to —

    (a) estimate the uncertainty in measurements

    (b) to make calculations in respect to chemical reactions

    (c) to calculate forces between the particles that make up the individual atoms, and between atoms, molecules and ions.

The scientific method is a name given to the process which has helped man to arrive at his present state of knowledge concerning the materials of which the world is made. This approach has a number of distinct steps —

    (i) observation of facts

    (ii) an hypothesis to explain the observed facts

    (iii) use of the hypothesis to suggest other consequences

    (iv) experiments to prove or disprove the suggested consequences and therefore —

    (v) establish or disprove the hypothesis

2. MATTER

Material is called matter by scientists. Matter is defined as anything which has inertia, (resistance to a change in direction or rate of motion), or has weight or occupies space.

Any sample of matter has been found to consist of one or more pure substances. A pure substance is one which always has the same composition no matter what its source or method of preparation. The number of pure substances which have been described is large but finite. Pure substances sometimes occur isolated in nature — for example, common salt, gold, quartz are pure substances. Usually natural materials are mixtures of pure substances — air, sea water, most rocks, soil, etc.

3. PROPERTIES
Properties are characteristics of pure substances which do not vary from sample to sample and therefore may be used to —
  (i) identify the pure substance or
  (ii) test for purity
Physical properties include state, colour, density, boiling point, melting point and electrical conductivity.

Chemical properties describe its behaviour in the presence of other pure substances under various stated conditions.

4. PURE SUBSTANCES — (Two Groups)
  (i) **Elements** — about 100 — substances which cannot be simplified by ordinary chemical methods. Elements contain only one kind of atom. An atom is the smallest particle of an element which retains all of the properties of that element. Examples of elements are oxygen, iron, copper, etc.

  (ii) **(Chemical) Compounds** — hundreds of thousands have been prepared and described. A compound is a pure substance composed of two or more elements combined in a definite (fixed) proportion by weight. For example, water is a compound which is always composed of 11.1% by weight hydrogen and 88.9% by weight oxygen.

Pure substances are always homogeneous, that is they have the same composition throughout — they are said to have only one phase.

5. PHYSICAL AND CHEMICAL CHANGES
Changes in pure substances are of two kinds —
  (i) **Physical change** — a change in state (solid, liquid, gas) or condition (temperature, pressure, etc.); which does not affect

the chemical composition. Ice melting, water evaporating, etc. are physical changes.

(ii) **Chemical changes—** a change in chemical composition; a different pure substance is produced. Examples of chemical changes are studied in I 6 Exp. (c) and (d).

6. EXPERIMENT (a) — To find the boiling point of methanol
Method — (i) Suspend a test tube containing 1 inch of methanol in a beaker of water. Suspend a thermometer in the methanol.
(ii) Heat water slowly and continue heating.

Observations —
(i) Temperature of methanol rises slowly to 66°C and remains stationary at 66°C.
(ii) Bubbles form in methanol at 66°C and rise to surface; this continues as the methanol boils away.

Conclusions —
(i) Boiling point of methanol is 66°C.
(ii) At the boiling point all the heat being added is used to change the liquid to vapour; this is the heat of vaporization for the liquid — for methanol it is 267 calories per gram.
(iii) Methanol (methyl alcohol) is a pure substance — it has a constant and definite boiling point. This is a physical change.

EXPERIMENT (b) — To find the melting point of naphthalene
Method —
(i) Place some naphthalene in a melting point tube and arrange as in Fig. 1.
(ii) Heat slowly to 85°C, then remove heat source and let cool. Repeat heating and cooling.

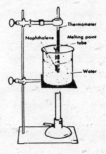

Fig. I — Finding a melting point.

Observations —

Temperature rises and naphthalene melts suddenly at 80°C. On cooling the naphthalene solidifies (freezes) at 80°C.

Conclusions —

Melting and freezing are physical changes. Naphthalene is a pure substance; it has a definite melting point which is the same as the freezing point of the liquid produced.

EXPERIMENT (c) — To study the decomposition of mercury (II) oxide

Method —

   (i)   weigh empty test tube with a plug of glass wool
   (ii) add some mercury (II) oxide and weigh again
   (iii) Heat slowly, then strongly; test with glowing splint
   (iv) Continue heating until no effect on splint
   (v) Cool and weigh again

Observations —

Mercury (II) oxide is an orange powder; it disappears slowly on heating; silvery droplets form on sides of test tube; splint ignites.

Conclusions —

Mercury (II) oxide is a compound which, on heating, decomposes into two elements — mercury (a silvery liquid) and oxygen (a colourless gas).

Weight of oxide used = method (ii) – (i)
Weight of oxygen given off = method (ii) – (v)

$$\% \text{ oxygen by weight} = \frac{\text{weight of oxygen}}{\text{weight of oxide}} \times 100$$

Within experimental error mercury (II) oxide should be
   7.4 % by weight oxygen
  82.6% by weight mercury
A number of samples should be done and the results compared.

EXPERIMENT (d) — To illustrate synthesis of compounds

(Synthesis is the building up of more complex from simpler substances.)

Method —

   (i) Warm a strip of copper foil and lower it into the vapour from boiling sulphur

(ii) Heat a mixture of zinc dust and flowers of sulphur in a test tube

Observations —

(i) Sulphur (an element) is a yellow solid which melts, turns dark reddish brown and boils at a high temperature. Copper (an element) is a reddish solid. Copper glows in sulphur vapour and becomes coated with a flaky black solid.

(ii) Zinc (an element) is a silvery grey solid. Zinc and sulphur mixture on heating gives off white fumes, a red flash occurs, white powder on sides of test tube.

Conclusions —

These processes are chemical reactions — compounds have formed from elements.

(i) copper + sulphur ⟶ copper (II) sulphide (black)

(ii) zinc + sulphur ⟶ zinc sulphide (white)

Properties of compounds are usually quite different from those of their constituent elements.

UNIT II: ATOMIC STRUCTURE

An atom is the smallest particle of an element which retains all of the properties of that element. The first real atomic theory was proposed by John Dalton in England in 1808 – his ideas with minor modifications are still considered to be correct. Symbols for elements are one or two letter abbreviations of the English name or of a Latinized name.

Names and symbols of the 20 elements which have the lightest atoms (least mass) are given in Fig. 2.

Atomic Number	Name	Symbol	Electron Configuration			
			K Shell	L Shell	M Shell	N Shell
1	Hydrogen	H	1			
2	Helium	He	2			
3	Lithium	Li	2	1		
4	Beryllium	Be	2	2		
5	Boron	B	2	3		
6	Carbon	C	2	4		
7	Nitrogen	N	2	5		
8	Oxygen	O	2	6		
9	Fluorine	F	2	7		
10	Neon	Ne	2	8		
11	Sodium	Na	2	8	1	
12	Magnesium	Mg	2	8	2	
13	Aluminium	Al	2	8	3	
14	Silicon	Si	2	8	4	
15	Phosphorus	P	2	8	5	
16	Sulphur	S	2	8	6	
17	Chlorine	Cl	2	8	7	
18	Argon	Ar	2	8	8	
19	Potassium	K	2	8	8	1
20	Calcium	Ca	2	8	8	2

Fig. 2 – The First Twenty Elements

I. FUNDAMENTAL PARTICLES

Three types of particles make up atoms; these particles were identified and studied chiefly by knocking them out of atoms by various types of projectiles.

(i) **Electron** – (J.J. Thomson 1897) – negatively charged particle with very small mass.

(ii) **Proton** – (Rutherford 1919) – a particle with charge equal and opposite to that of the electron; its mass about 1840 times that of the electron.

(iii) **Neutron** – (Chadwick 1932) – an uncharged particle of mass approximately equal to that of the proton.

This may be summed up as follows –

Particle	Relative Mass	Relative Charge
Electron	$\dfrac{1}{1840}$	–1
Proton	1	+1
Neutron	1	0

The mass of the atom is therefore due almost entirely to protons and neutrons; if we assign a mass of unity (1 atomic mass unit) to each of these, the number of neutrons plus the number of protons in atoms gives us numbers which serve as a scale of relative atomic masses.

The dimensions and actual masses of these particles have been found.—

Particle	Mass	Diameter
electron	9.11×10^{-28} grams	5.6×10^{-13} cm.
proton	1.672×10^{-24} grams	1×10^{-13} cm.
neutron	1.675×10^{-24} grams	

2. THE ATOM

(a) **The Nuclear Atom** – Rutherford (1911) – from results of experiments in which he bombarded gold foil, approximately 10,000 atoms thick, with charged helium atoms (alpha particles), proposed the following concept of the atom –

(i) the atom occupies a spherical volume of about 10^{-8} cm. radius.

(ii) each atom has at its centre a very dense nucleus of about 10^{-12} cm. radius.

(iii) the nucleus contains most of the mass of the atom.

(iv) the nucleus has a positive charge which is some multiple of the charge on the electron.

(v) the electrons are in orbit around the nucleus.

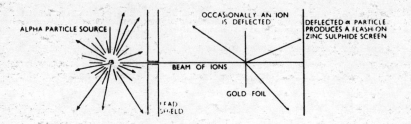

Fig. 3 — Rutherford's Discovery of the Nucleus

The above concept describes a planetary atom in which the force of attraction between an electron and the protons in the nucleus is balanced by the outward force due to the movement of the electron in its orbit.

The forces which hold the protons together in the nucleus have not been clearly explained.

If an atomic nucleus were magnified to the size of a golf ball, the electrons would be about the size of tennis balls at distances of the order of a mile; the nucleus would then weigh thousands of tons.

(b) Atomic Number and Mass Number

The nucleus is now known to consist of protons and neutrons; the number of protons is the "atomic number" — this also gives the nuclear charge in positive units. The protons and neutrons together make up most of the mass of the atom and the sum of their number is the "mass number" of the nucleus. If the atom is neutral the number of electrons is the same as the number of protons. Atom identification and composition may be given by using the symbol of the element with the mass number as a superscript and the atomic number as a subscript — e.g. $_{17}Cl^{35}$ stands for a chlorine atom whose nucleus has 17 protons and 18 neutrons and which has 17 electrons (see electron arrangement in following section).

(c) Electron Arrangement

Scientists now think of the space around the nucleus in an atom as being filled with negative electricity due to rapidly moving electrons and they refer to an electron charge cloud instead of an orbit. The electrons have different energies and are thought of as being in different energy levels or shells. The shells are called K, L, M, N etc; the K shell nearest the nucleus having the lowest energy. It has been established that the maximum number of electrons possible in each shell is $2n^2$ where "n" is the number of the shell (k = 1).

	Shell No.	Max. No. of Electrons
i.e.	1 (K)	2
	2 (L)	8
	3 (M)	18
	4 (N)	32 etc.

The electron arrangements in the elements with atomic numbers 1-20 are given in Fig. 2; these are shown diagrammatically in Fig. 4 (except Al and Si).

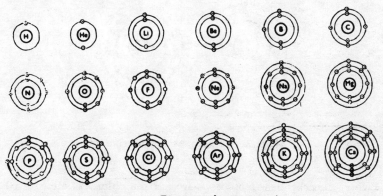

Fig. 4 — Electron Arrangement

(d) Schematic diagrams for atoms may be drawn from mass number and atomic number as indicated in Fig. 5.

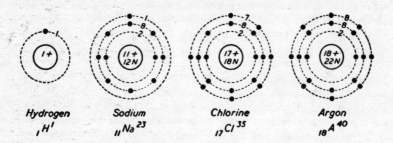

Fig. 5 — Atom Composition Diagrams

(e) Isotopes

Atoms of an element have the same atomic number (same number of protons) but they may have different masses because of different numbers of neutrons; these are called isotopes. For example chlorine consists of two isotopes of mass numbers 35 and 37 —

$_{17}Cl^{35}$ and $_{17}Cl^{37}$ — these are shown in Fig. 6

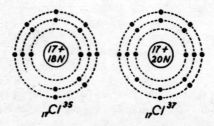

Fig. 6 — Isotopes of Chlorine

Every element has isotopes — from 2 in chlorine, etc. to 10 in tin.

The relative abundance of the isotopic forms of an element in nature is very nearly constant; for example chlorine always contains 3 atoms of mass number 35 to 1 atom of mass number 37 or carbon in nature always consists of 99 atoms of $_6C^{12}$ to 1 atom of $_6C^{13}$

Isotopes have identical chemical properties but their physical properties differ somewhat because of their mass difference.

(f) Atomic Weight

It has been pointed out that most of the mass of the atom is concentrated in the nucleus and that the isotopes of an element have different nuclear masses. Masses of atoms can be compared to the mass of any given atom. Oxygen was for many years used as a standard for establishing a relative mass scale for atoms. In 1961 scientists began to use the carbon 12 isotope ($_6C^{12}$) as the standard. An atomic mass unit (a.m.u.) is defined as $\frac{1}{12}$ of the mass of an atom of $_6C^{12}$ (this unit is obviously very close to the mass of a proton or of a neutron – it has a value of 1.66×10^{-24} grams). For most calculations the weighted average of the atomic masses of the isotopes of an element is used as the atomic mass – this is the "atomic weight" of the element and is in atomic mass units. The atomic weight, since it is an average, is usually not a whole number. For example the atomic weight of chlorine is 35.5 since there are 3 atoms of mass 35 to 1 atom of mass 37.

For purposes of calculation we usually express the relative weights of atoms in grams and call them gram-atomic weights.

3. ION STRUCTURE

An ion is an atom which has lost or gained one or more electrons and therefore has one or more positive or negative charges.

(a) The Inert Gases

A family of elements including helium, neon and argon (see unit II, 2c) are considered to have stable electron arrangements since they do not undergo any change in electron structure to enter into chemical reaction – they are called inert gases. The inactivity of these inert gases is thought to be due to complete outer electron shells – 2 in the K shell or 8 in L, M, N etc. shells. The chemical activity of the more reactive elements is thought to be due to their tendency to lose or gain electrons

16

to become ions with the electron configuration of the nearest inert gas.

(b) Formation of Ions
Active metals usually have 1 or 2 electrons in the outer shell (e.g. Na or Ca); these can be readily lost to form positive ions (Na^+ or Ca^{2+}), which have a stable octet of electrons in the outer shell.

Metals are said to be electro positive.

Active non-metals usually have 6 or 7 electrons in the outer shell and must gain 1 or 2 electrons to become negative ions with a stable outer octet. (e.g. Cl becomes Cl^- and O becomes O^{2-}).

Non-metals are electro negative.

In compound formation these oppositely charged ions are held together by electrostatic attraction.

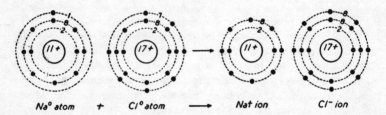

Na^0 atom $+$ Cl^0 atom $\longrightarrow$ Na^+ ion Cl^- ion

Fig. 7 — Formation of Sodium Chloride

In Fig. 7 the sodium ion (Na^+) has the same electron configuration as Neon and the chloride ion (Cl-) has the electron configuration of argon.

Ions are formed only by atoms which are active enough to give up or accept electrons.

UNIT III: THE STRUCTURE OF AGGREGATES OF ATOMS

In nature atoms usually occur in aggregations with other atoms, held together by forces called chemical bonds. Exceptions to this are the inert gases (helium, neon etc.) in which the atoms are isolated.

There are four types of atom groups —
    (i)   ionic crystals
    (ii) molecules
    (iii) covalent crystals
    (iv) metals

I. IONIC CRYSTALS

Ions formed by electron transfer are held together by a bond which is the attraction between unlike charges; the substances formed are ionic (electrovalent) compounds. In the solid state these compounds consist of crystals constructed of the ions arranged in a regular pattern which repeats itself over and over again.

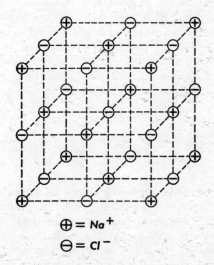

$\oplus = Na^+$

$\ominus = Cl^-$

Fig. 8 — Crystal Lattice Structure of Sodium Chloride

In a crystal a positive ion is not associated with any one particular negative ion; the bonds are quite strong so that the melting point is high;

When the solid is melted the ions are free to move.

The crystal is electrically neutral since the relationship between numbers of ions and charges on ions is always such that the total number of positive charges equals the total number of negative charges.

Combinations of symbols called formulas are used to represent compounds. The formula gives the relative numbers of ions — for example NaCl (or Na^+Cl^-) means a 1 to 1 ratio of ions or $CaCl_2$ ($Ca^{2+}2Cl^-$) means a 1 to 2 ratio etc.

The charge on the ion is called the electrovalence (or ionic valence) of the element; for example in the above illustration chlorine has an electrovalence of -1 and calcium an electrovalence of +2.

The term valence may be simply defined as the combining capacity of an element.

2. MOLECULES

A molecule may be defined as the smallest particle of a substance having all of the properties of that substance; this definition could apply to both elements and compounds. The ionic compounds mentioned above are not considered to have molecules. Molecules are groups of atoms held together by a different kind of bond, which is called the covalent bond. Formulas are used to represent molecules — here the formula gives the actual number of atoms of each element in the molecule; molecules of elements have only one kind of atom. Examples of molecules are — H_2 (hydrogen), HF (hydrogen fluoride), NH_3 (ammonia), $CHCl_3$ (chloroform), etc.

The covalent bond is formed by sharing electrons between two atoms. The shared electrons are attracted simultaneously by the 2 positive nuclei and this evidently establishes a stable energy condition; it is a force holding the atoms together since work has to be done to separate them. Electrons are usually shared in pairs, one from each atom, in order to acquire the stable octet of electrons in the outer shell (2 if only 1 shell). One pair of shared electrons is called a covalent bond and is represented in a formula by a pair of dots or a dash — for example H : Cl or H – Cl.

Covalent bonding may be shown by diagrams —

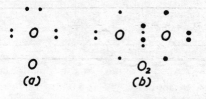

O
(a)

O_2
(b)

Fig. 9 — The Oxygen Molecule
Here only the outer electron shell is shown.

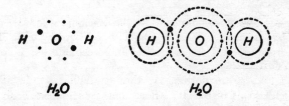

H_2O

H_2O

Fig. 10 — The Water Molecule

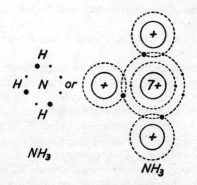

NH_3

NH_3

Fig. 11 — The Ammonia Molecule

From Figs. 9, 10, 11 it is evident that an atom may form more than one covalent bond — e.g. nitrogen in ammonia forms three. If more than one pair of shared electrons form the bond between two atoms the bond is called a double or triple bond — for example —

(a) $H_2C = CH_2$ (ethylene) has a double bond (2 shared electrons pairs) between the two carbon atoms.

(b) $O = C = O$ (carbon dioxide) has a double bond between C and each O.

(c) $H - C \equiv C - H$ (acetylene) has a triple bond (3 shared electron pairs) between the two carbon atoms.

(d) $N \equiv N$ (nitrogen molecule) has a triple bond between the two nitrogen atoms.

The above formulas are usually written simply —

C_2H_4 ; CO_2 ; C_2H_2 ; N_2

The covalence of an element is the number of covalent bonds formed by an atom of that element — e.g. nitrogen in ammonia has a covalence of 3 or carbon in carbon dioxide has a covalence of 4 etc.

3. COVALENT CRYSTALS (sometimes called network solids)

These are crystals whose particles are held together by covalent bonds. Examples are —

(a) Diamond — an element (carbon) in which each carbon atom is surrounded by 4 others to which it is covalently bonded, forming a compact, very hard structure.

(b) Silica — (quartz - SiO_2) — covalent bonds again produce a very hard substance.

These crystals contain large numbers of atoms — the name molecule is not appropriate.

The formula here (e.g. SiO_2) simply gives the ratio in which the atoms are present but does not describe a molecule.

4. METALS — consist of crystals made of millions of atoms held together by free electrons moving among positive ions. This situation exists because the valence electrons are not strongly held and, since they are approximately the same distance from two or more positive nuclei, they move freely throughout the crystal. The mobile electrons account for some of the properties of metals —

for example —

(i)   they carry an electric current through the metal

(ii) they carry heat readily in the form of kinetic energy

(iii) metallic bonding is strong and therefore metals have high strength and high melting points

(iv) the plane surfaces of the crystals give metals their characteristic properties of light reflection which we call metallic lustre.

UNIT IV: STATES OF MATTER

Matter exists in 3 states — solid, liquid and gas.
Study of these states must take into account the following —

(i) nature of the particles of which it is composed — atoms, ions or molecules

(ii) forces between the particles — electrostatic or van der Waal's forces (attraction between electrons of one atom and nucleus of another)

(iii) motion of particles — translational (through space from one position to another), vibrational (back and forth about a fixed point) or rotational (spinning around a fixed centre).

(iv) effect of collisions of particles — loss of energy etc.

(v) distance apart of particles — this affects forces, frequency of collisions, etc.

I. SOLIDS

(a) Structural particles may be —
(i) similar atoms — copper, diamond

(ii) different atoms — quartz (SiO_2)

(iii) molecules — ice (H_2O), Sulphur (S_8)

(iv) ions — sodium chloride (Na^+ and Cl^-)

(b) Forces between particles —
(i) van der Waal's (usually weak) e.g. sugar

(ii) electrostatic — if ions e.g. NaCl

(iii) covalent — e.g. metals

Electrostatic and covalent forces are usually quite strong and give the solid a high melting point.

(c) Motion of particles is only vibrational and therefore at a given temperature the shape and volume are definite. Distance between particles is very small, hence the solid is almost incompressible.

Temperature is a measure of the average kinetic energy of the particles; increase in temperature increases velocity of particles and therefore vibrational energy, more vigorous collisions force particles farther apart and an increase in volume results.

(d) Melting point

At a certain temperature the particles begin translational movement — they slip past each other and the substance becomes a liquid. Melting point (or freezing point) is the temperature at which solid and liquid states can exist together in equilibrium (at a pressure of 1 atmosphere).

(e) Heat of fusion is the energy which has to be added to the solid (or removed from the liquid) to cause the change in state at the melting (freezing) point. This energy is usually given in calories of heat per gram of substance — e.g.

Substance	Heat of Fusion
	cal/gram
ice	80
copper	42
lead	5.9

When the substance melts this heat of fusion is changed into molecular kinetic energy which is released again as heat if the substance freezes.

(f) Sublimation

Molecules in a solid which acquire higher than average kinetic energy may escape from the attractive forces of molecules at the surface of the solid and form a vapour (gas); this process is called sublimation as is also the reverse process

$$(gas \longrightarrow solid)$$

Some familiar examples are —
  (i)   dry ice disappears
  (ii) frozen clothes dry
  (iii) snow crystals form
  (iv) moth crystals disappear

Experiment — to show sublimation

  (i) Immerse a test tube containing a crystal of iodine in boiling water for a few minutes — remove and observe.

  (ii) Place some benzoic acid on a watch glass; cover with a filter paper; invert a second watch glass over the filter paper; warm gently well above a flame.

(g) Non-crystalline (amorphous) solids

Some solids have no definite crystal shape (no orderly particle arrangement) — when fractured they do not show plane surfaces or definite angles between surfaces. Examples of these are glass and plastics. When the liquid state of such a solid is cooled it gradually increases in viscosity (resistance to flow) until it appears to be solid — there is no definite freezing point. The amorphous form may be unstable — glass for example will crystallize under certain conditions. These substances are sometimes called supercooled liquids.

2. LIQUIDS

(a) **Particles** may be atoms (mercury), molecules (water) or ions (fused sodium chloride).

(b) **Motion of particles** translational as well as vibrational and rotational — particles still essentially in contact. The volume is definite at a given temperature but the shape is indefinite; the substance is almost imcompressible. Volume, and therefore density, almost the same as the solid.

(c) **Rise in temperature** increases average speed and therefore average kinetic energy of particles, forces them farther apart and increases volume.

(d) Vaporization

At the surface of a liquid some particles with much greater than average kinetic energy escape from the attraction of the other particles and become vapour (gas); this is vaporization (evaporation). Rate of evaporation increases with rise in temperature. As particles with higher energies escape, the average kinetic energy decreases and the temperature of the liquid drops — energy must be added to keep the temperature constant. Heat of vaporization is the energy required to change liquid to vapour at a constant temperature; these are given in calories per gram — e.g.

Substance	Heat of Vaporization cal/gram
water	540
alcohol	205
benzene	93
ether	88

Heat of vaporization is released as the vapour condenses. A liquid has a heat of vaporization at any temperature — it varies somewhat with temperature and is usually given at the boiling point.

(e) Vapour pressure

If a liquid evaporates into a closed space at a fixed temperature, the gas particles begin to be recaptured at the liquid surface (condensation). When rates of condensation and evaporation are the same an equilibrium exists and at this condition the pressure exerted by the gas is called the vapour pressure of the liquid at that particular temperature. Vapour is the name used for the gaseous state of a substance which is liquid or solid at room temperature.

Pressure exerted by a gas is due to collisions between the particles and the enclosing walls. As temperature rises rate of evaporation rises and vapour pressure rises. Solids also have vapour pressure.

If a liquid is heated in an open vessel its temperature and vapour pressure rise until the vapour pressure is equal to the atmosphere pressure — at this point bubbles of vapour form in the body of the liquid — this temperature is the Boiling Point of the liquid: boiling point may be defined as the temperature at which the vapour pressure of the liquid = 760 mm. Addition of heat at the boiling point does not raise the temperature — it is all used to vaporize the liquid. High boiling points of metals (Fe = 2450°C) are due to strong metallic bonds. Low boiling points of molecular substances (H_2O = 100°C) are due to small van der Waal's forces between the molecules.

(f) Experiment — to illustrate vapour pressure

Set up mercury barometers as in Fig. 12. Measure lengths of mercury columns. Introduce liquid water and chloroform (or benzene) as in diagram so that a small amount of the liquid remains on the surface of the mercury when equilibrium has been established. Decrease in length of mercury column = vapour pressure of liquid at that temperature.

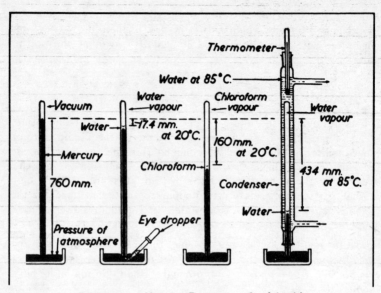

Fig. 12 — Vapour Pressure of a Liquid

3. GASES

(a) **Particles** are molecules or atoms relatively far apart; their motion is mainly translational. A gas occupies the entire volume of the container — i.e. it has no definite volume or shape; it can be greatly compressed; gas densities are low compared with liquids or solids.

(b) Kinetic-Molecular Theory

This theory can be applied to all states of matter but is most useful in its application to account for the behaviour of gases in respect to heat and pressure. The main postulates of this theory are —

(i) a gas consists of many small identical particles relatively far apart.

(ii) the particles are in continuous rapid, random motion; they collide with each other and with the walls of the container. The pressure of the gas is due to this bombardment.

(iii) the particles are perfectly elastic — no loss in energy on colliding.

(c) Diffusion is the process by which particles of a gas spread through space; this is due to their straight line translational motion with frequent collisions with other particles producing zig-zag paths.

At a fixed temperature particles of all gases have the same average kinetic energy (K.E. = $\frac{1}{2}mv^2$) where "m" is the mass and "v" is the average speed.

For gas A and gas B at the same temperature —

$\frac{1}{2}m_A(v_A)^2 = \frac{1}{2}m_B(v_B)^2$ which reduces to —

$$\frac{\sqrt{m_A}}{\sqrt{m_B}} = \frac{v_B}{v_A}$$ (i.e. speeds of particles are inversely proportional to the square roots of their masses.)

Rates of diffusion should be approximately proportional to speeds of particles and therefore inversely proportional to square roots of particles masses (Graham's Law).

Experiment — To compare rates of diffusion
Method

(i) Fix horizontally an open ended glass tube approximately 15" long and 1" diameter.

(ii) Place simultaneously in ends of tube two stoppers to which are pinned balls of absorbent cotton soaked in HCl and NH_3 solutions.

(iii) Measure position of ring of white smoke which appears after a short time.

Observations

In a typical experiment the white smoke (NH_4Cl) appears 5" from HCl end and 7.5" from NH_3 end.

Conclusion

Gases HCl and NH_3 are released from the solutions and diffuse through the air in the tube; NH_3 diffuses faster than HCl.

$$\frac{\text{particle mass of } NH_3}{\text{particle mass of HCl}} = \frac{17}{36.5}$$

$\frac{\sqrt{17}}{\sqrt{36.5}}$ approximately $= \frac{5}{7.5}$ ($\therefore$ rates of diffusion are inversely proportional to square roots of particle masses).

Speed of gas particles is also greater at higher temperature — it is approximately proportional to $\sqrt{K}$, where K is the temperature on the Absolute (Kelvin) scale; on this scale the zero point (Absolute zero) is –273°C and at this temperature molecular motion is assumed to stop. (°K = °C + 273)

(d) Avogadro's Principle – Equal volumes of gases at the same temperature and pressure contain equal numbers of molecules. This was first suggested in 1811 as a hypothesis to explain observations on combining volumes of gases; it is now accepted as a principle (or law).

(e) Boyle's Law – If the temperature is kept constant the volume of a given mass of gas varies inversely as the pressure.

(i) Experiment to illustrate Boyle's Law

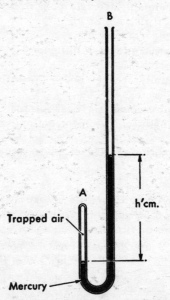

Fig. 13 — Effect of pressure on gas volume

Using the apparatus in Fig. 13, vary the pressure on the trapped gas (air) by changing the level of mercury in the tube B; the pressure on the trapped air is equal to atmospheric pressure plus the pressure exerted by h'cm. of mercury. Make several measurements of pressure (P) and corresponding volume (V) and for each calculate $P \times V$. It is found that, if the temperature remains constant, $PV = $ a constant.

Boyle's Law may be written $P_1V_1 = P_2V_2$ (if temperature and mass of gas remain the same)

or $V_2 = V_1 \times \dfrac{P_1}{P_2}$

(ii) Explanation of Boyle's Law

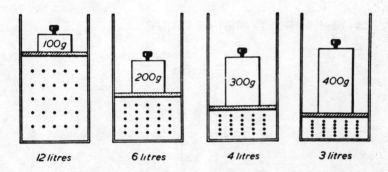

Fig. 14 — Effect of Pressure on gas volume

In Fig. 14 it is evident that if the volume of the gas is halved the concentration of particles is twice as great and therefore they will hit a unit area of wall surface twice as often as before. If the temperature is constant there will be the same force per collision (average kinetic energy constant), therefore the pressure of the gas will be twice as great.

(f) Charles' Law

(i) The French chemist, Charles, found that any gas expands or contracts $\frac{1}{273}$ of its volume at 0°C for each centigrade degree rise or fall in temperature. This led to the formation of a temperature scale called the Kelvin (or Absolute) scale on which 0°K = –273°C and 0°C = 273°K (i.e. °K = °C + 273).

If we let the volume of a certain mass of gas at 0°C be V_0, its volume at 0°K would be $V_0 - \frac{273}{273} V_0$ which equals zero; gases however liquify before reaching 0°K and this relationship does not hold for liquids. At 273°C this volume would be $V_0 + \frac{273}{273} V_0$ or $2V_0$.

Charles' Law

The volume of a quantity of gas, kept at constant pressure, varies directly as the absolute (Kelvin) temperature; (i.e. the volumes at different temperatures are directly proportional to the Absolute temperatures.)

For example: $\dfrac{\text{Volume at 50°C}}{\text{Volume at 100°C}} = \dfrac{273 + 50}{273 + 100} = \dfrac{323}{373}$

(ii) Experiment – To illustrate Charles' Law

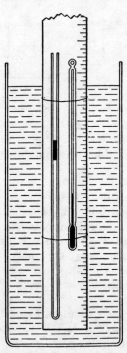

Fig. 15 – Effect of temperature on gas volume

In the apparatus in Fig. 15 the bead of mercury traps a certain mass of gas (air) in a glass tube. As the temperature in the surrounding bath is raised the volume of the gas is seen to increase. If the bore of the tube is uniform the volumes of the gas are proportional to the lengths of the tube they occupy. The pressure on the gas is constant (atmospheric).

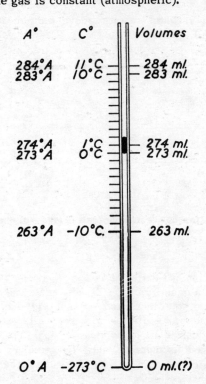

Fig. 16 — Temperature and volume relationship in a gas

Fig. 16 shows observations made if the mass of gas taken has a volume of exactly 273 ml. at 0°C. These volumes are directly proportional to the Absolute temperatures. A series of measurements should be made with any fixed mass of gas and the values of $\dfrac{V}{T}$ calculated (T = °K).

It is found that $\dfrac{V}{T}$ = a constant.

or $\dfrac{V_1}{T_1} = \dfrac{V_2}{T_2}$ or $V_2 = V_1 \times \dfrac{T_2}{T_1}$

This relationship is Charles' Law.

(iii) The experimental results above can be illustrated graphically as in Fig. 17.

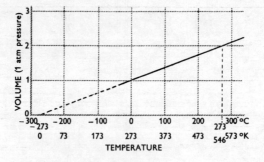

Fig. 17 — Relation between temperature and volume of a sample of gas

(iv) Explanation of Charles' Law

If the volume of a quantity of gas is kept the same, as the temperature increases, the increased pressure is due to increased number of collisions of particles with the walls of the container and increased change in momentum at each collision. If the volume is allowed to increase until the pressure is the same as before, the relationship $V = kT$ can be mathematically deduced from the above effects.

(g) Example Problems

In order to more easily compare gas volumes and densities scientists use a standard pressure (760 mm. of mercury) and a standard temperature (0°C); these conditions are referred to as S.T.P. (standard temperature and pressure). A pressure of 760 mm. of mercury means a pressure sufficient to hold up a column of mercury 760 mm. long; this is also called 1 atmosphere and is approximately 14.7 lbs. per sq. in.

Problem 1: (Volume, density and pressure at constant temperature)
A certain quantity of gas has a volume of 2 litres (l) at S.T.P.
and weighs 2.86 grams (g).

(a) Find its density in grams per litre (g.p.l.) at S.T.P.

(b) Find its volume if the pressure is increased to 1140 mm.
(temperature remaining at 0°C)

(c) Find the density of the gas at the conditions in (b).

Solution:

(a) 1 l. of gas at S.T.P. weighs $\dfrac{2.86 \text{ g}}{2} = 1.43$ grams

∴ its density = 1.43 g.p.l.

(b) $V_2 = V_1 \times \dfrac{P_2}{P_1}$ (Boyle's Law)

$V_2 = 2 \text{ litres} \times \dfrac{1140 \text{ mm.}}{760 \text{ mm.}} = 3 \text{ l.}$ (3000 ml.)

(c) 3 l. at 1140 mm. pressure and 0°C weigh 2.86 g.

∴ 1 l. at 1140 mm. and 0°C weighs $\dfrac{2.86 \text{ g}}{3} = 0.95$ g.

Density = 0.95 g.p.l.

Problem 2: (Volume, density and temperature at constant pressure
A gas (chlorine) has a density of 3.26 g.p.l. at S.T.P.

(a) Find the volume of 9.78 g. of this gas at a pressure
1 atmosphere and a temperature of 182°C.

(b) Find the density of this gas (in g.p.l.) at 182°C and
pressure of 1 atmosphere.

Solution:

(a) 3.26 g. of gas at 0°C and 1 atmosphere occupy 1 l.

∴ 9.78 g. of gas at S.T.P. occupy $\dfrac{9.78 \text{ g.}}{3.26 \text{ g.}} \times 1 \text{ l.} = 3 \text{ l.}$

$V_2 = V_1 \times \dfrac{T_2}{T_1}$ (Charles' Law)

∴ Volume at 1 atmosphere and 182°C =

$3 \text{ litres} \times \dfrac{455°K}{273°K} = 5 \text{ l.}$

(b) At 1 atmosphere and 182°C, 5 l. of gas weigh 9.78 g.

∴ at 1 atmosphere and 182°C, 1 l. of gas weighs

$$\frac{1 \text{ l.}}{5 \text{ l.}} \times 9.78 \text{ g.} = 1.96 \text{ g.}$$

∴ Density = 1.96 g.p.l.

Problem 3: (Volume and density with temperature and pressure changing)

A gas (oxygen) has a density of 1.43 g.p.l. at S.T.P.

(a) Find the volume of 5.0 g. of oxygen at 2 atmospheres pressure and 91°C.

(b) Find the density of oxygen at the temperature and pressure in (a).

Solution:

(a) Combining Boyle's and Charles' Laws —

$$V_2 = V_1 \times \frac{P_1}{P_2} \times \frac{T_2}{T_1}$$

1.43 g. at S.T.P. occupy a volume of 1.0 l.

∴ 5.0 g. at S.T.P. occupy $\dfrac{5.0 \text{ g.}}{1.43 \text{ g.}} \times 1 \text{ l.} = 3.5 \text{ l.}$

Volume at 2 atmospheres and 91°C

$$= 3.5 \text{ l.} \times \frac{1 \text{ at.}}{2 \text{ at.}} \times \frac{364°K}{273°K} = 2.3 \text{ l.}$$

(b) 2.3 l. at 2 atm. pressure and 91°C weigh 5.0 g.

∴ 1.0 l. at 2 atm. and 91°C weigh

$$\frac{1.0 \text{ l.}}{2.3 \text{ l.}} \times 5.0 \text{ g} = 2.2 \text{ g}$$

∴ Density = 2.2 g.p.l. (at 2 atm. and 91°C)

UNIT V: VALENCE, FORMULAS, NOMENCLATURE AND EQUATIONS

I. FORMULAS AND NOMENCLATURE

(a) In Unit II names and symbols of some common elements were used. A formula is a group of symbols which represents a chemical compound and gives its composition. If the compound is ionic the formula, e.g. NaCl, represents —

(i) ratio of atoms — i.e. 1 sodium atom to 1 chlorine atom

(ii) ratio by weight — i.e. 23 weight units of sodium to 35.5 weight units of chlorine

If the compound is molecular the formula, which is then called the molecular formula, e.g. C_2H_2 (acetylene), gives the same information as above and also gives the actual number of atoms of each element in the molecule.

Binary compounds contain 2 elements; in naming these the name of the positive ion (or more electropositive element) is placed first and followed by the negative ion with the name changed to end in "ide" — for example

NaCl	sodium chloride
MgO	magnesium oxide
K_2S	potassium sulphide
CaH_2	calcium hydride

(b) **Radicals** are groups of atoms which tend to stay together and go through reactions as a unit; they are held together by covalent bonds but are usually compound ions with an overall charge. These radicals when combined with hydrogen form compounds called acids — see table below.

Radical Name	Ion Formula	Acid Formula	Acid Name
sulphate	SO_4^{2-}	H_2SO_4	sulphuric
sulphite	SO_3^{2-}	H_2SO_3	sulphurous
nitrate	NO_3^-	HNO_3	Nitric
nitrite	NO_2^-	HNO_2	nitrous
phosphate	PO_4^{3-}	H_3PO_4	phosphoric
phosphite	PO_3^{3-}	H_3PO_3	phosphorous
chlorate	ClO_3^-	$HClO_3$	chloric
chlorite	ClO_2^-	$HClO_2$	chlorous
carbonate	CO_3^{2-}	H_2CO_3	carbonic

Acids are covalent compounds.
Note that radicals ending in "ate" form acids ending in "ic" and radicals ending in "ite" form acids ending in "ous".

(c) **A salt** is an ionic compound formed by replacing the hydrogen of an acid by a metal — it is referred to as a salt of the corresponding acid. For example Na_2SO_4 (sodium sulphate) is the sodium salt of sulphuric acid or $CaCO_3$ (calcium carbonate) is the calcium salt of carbonic acid, etc.
The acids can be named as hydrogen compounds — e.g. H_2SO_4 (sulphuric acid) is hydrogen sulphate.

(d) **Two other common radicals** which form ions are —
(i) ammonium (NH_4+) which acts as a metal forming salts — e.g. $(NH_4)_2SO_4$ — ammonium sulphate, etc. and
(ii) hydroxide ($OH-$) which combines with metals forming compounds called bases which have properties opposite to acids — e.g. NaOH — sodium hydroxide
$Ca(OH)_2$ — calcium hydroxide, etc.

2. VALENCE

(a) **Atomic structure and valence** — In Unit III valence was simply defined as the combining capacity of an element. This combining capacity was shown to be due to loosely bound electrons in the outer shell — the so called valence electrons. These electrons are given up, received or shared during formation of compounds. Valence is often defined as the number of atoms of hydrogen with which an atom will combine or which it will release in a chemical reaction.

(b) **Kinds of valence** — In Unit III two kinds were mentioned and defined —
(i) Electrovalence — the charge on the ion formed in an ionic bond
(ii) Covalence — the number of shared pairs of electrons (covalent bonds formed)

(c) **Valence Table** — The following table gives electro valences for common elements and compound ions.

Atomic Number	Name	Symbol	Valence
I	Hydrogen	H	1+ (1– in metal hydrides)
3	Lithium	Li	1+
7	Nitrogen	N	3+ or 5+ (3– in NH_3)
8	Oxygen	O	2–
11	Sodium	Na	1+
12	Magnesium	Mg	2+
13	Aluminium	Al	3+
15	Phosphorus	P	3+ or 5+
16	Sulphur	S	4+ or 6+ (2– in sulphides)
17	Chlorine	Cl	1– (in chlorides)
19	Potassium	K	1+
20	Calcium	Ca	2+
26	Iron	Fe	2+ or 3+
29	Copper	Cu	1+ or 2+
30	Zinc	Zn	2+
35	Bromine	Br	1– (in bromides)
47	Silver	Ag	1+
53	Iodine	I	1– (in iodides)
56	Barium	Ba	2+
80	Mercury	Hg	1+ or 2+
82	Lead	Pb	2+ or 4+

RADICALS

Name	Ion Formula	Valence
Hydroxide	OH^-	1–
Chlorate	ClO_3^-	1–
Chlorite	ClO_2^-	1–
Nitrate	NO_3^-	1–
Nitrite	NO_2^-	1–
Sulphate	SO_4^{2-}	2–
Sulphite	SO_3^{2-}	2–
Phosphate	PO_4^{3-}	3–
Phosphite	PO_3^{3-}	3–
Carbonate	CO_3^{2-}	2–
Ammonium	NH_4^+	1+

3. WRITING FORMULAS AND NAMES

(a) **Formulas from names** – Certain rules for naming compounds were given in Unit V 1. In writing a formula the atoms or radicals must be combined in relative numbers so that the sum of the valences = 0.

e.g.   sodium oxide Na_2O (i.e. $2Na^+ . O^{2-}$)

aluminium sulphide Al_2S_3 ($2Al^{3+} . 3S^{2-}$)

calcium nitrate $Ca(NO_3)_2$ ($Ca^{2+} . 2NO_3^{1-}$)

(b) **Names from formulas** – A compound can be named from the formula, using the same rules as above. Valences can be determined from formulas. Some elements have more than one valence and therefore form more than one compound with another element. For example iron forms 2 chlorides $FeCl_2$ and $FeCl_3$; the valence of chlorine in chlorides is 1–, therefore iron must be 2+ in $FeCl_2$ and 3+ in $FeCl_3$. There are three methods of naming used to distinguish the compounds in cases like this –

	$FeCl_2$	$FeCl_3$
(i) a prefix	iron dichloride	iron trichloride

(ii) a Roman numeral
      for valence   iron (II) chloride   iron (III) chloride

(iii) the ending "ous"
      for lower valence   ferrous chloride   ferric chloride
      "ic" for higher
      valence.

Method (ii) above is preferred.

4. A CHEMICAL REACTION is a process involving the re-arrangement of atoms of one or more substances (reactants) so that one or more new substances (products) are produced. This is always accompanied by a release or absorption of energy (usually in the form of heat). An exothermic reaction gives off energy as it goes on (the products have less energy than the reactants). An endothermic reaction absorbs energy as it goes on (the products have more energy than the reactants).

5. A CHEMICAL EQUATION represents a chemical reaction; the formulas for reactants on the left side of the arrow and the formulas for products on the right side.

Balancing an equation is making any changes necessary so that there is the same number of each kind of atom on both sides of the equation (law of conservation of mass). Balancing can only be done by changing coefficients (never subscripts since this would change the formula). For example the laboratory preparation of oxygen can be described by the following equation —

$$KClO_3 \longrightarrow O_2 + KCl \text{ (not balanced)}$$

or $2KClO_3 \longrightarrow 3O_2 + 2KCl$ (balanced)

A balanced equation gives the following information about a reaction —

(i)   identifies reactants and products
(ii) gives correct composition of each reactant and product
(iii) gives relative numbers of atoms or molecules involved
(iv) gives relative weights of substances involved

Calculations from equations are explained in Unit IX.

UNIT VI: OXYGEN

I. NATURAL OCCURRENCE — About 6 out of every 10 atoms in the earth's crust are oxygen. It occurs uncombined in air (about 21% by volume); combined in oxides, carbonates, silicates, etc. in rocks and soil (about 50%); in complex compounds, carbohydrates, fats, proteins, etc. in living organisms (about 65%); in water 89%.

Oxygen is removed from air by processes such as respiration and decay but is returned to the air by photosynthesis carried on by green plants.

$$(6CO_2 + 6H_2O \longrightarrow C_6H_{12}O_6 \text{ (sugar)} + 6O_2)$$

so that the % of O_2 in air remains the same.

2. LABORATORY PREPARATION
(a) Heating Oxides
e.g. $2HgO \longrightarrow 2Hg + O_2$ (Unit I Exp. (c))

(b) Heating Chlorates
EXPERIMENT — The effect of manganese dioxide (MnO_2) on the decomposition of potassium chlorate ($KClO_3$)
Method —

Heat 1 cm. of $KClO_3$ in a test tube, gently then strongly, testing with a glowing splint. Repeat, heating $KClO_3$ just to melting, remove from heat, add a pinch of MnO_2 and test with glowing splint. Continue heating until no further effect on splint; cool, add H_2O, shake, filter, dry residue. Repeat experiment using residue in place of MnO_2.

Observations —

$KClO_3$ melts to colorless liquid; no effect on splint until strongly heated, then colorless gas bubbles and splint ignites. MnO_2 causes bubbling and ignition of splint just above melting point. Black residue left on filter paper acts the same as MnO_2.

Conclusion —

$KClO_3$ decomposes on heating to produce O_2 and a white solid with a higher melting point than $KClO_3$. This decomposition is speeded up by MnO_2 which is not permanently changed during the reaction (same weight can be recovered).

$$2KClO_3 \xrightarrow{MnO_2} 2KCl + 3O_2$$

MnO_2 is a catalyst for this reaction.

A catalyst is a substance which changes the rate of a chemical reaction and is not itself permanently changed.

The laboratory production and collection of oxygen from $KClO_3$ is shown in Fig. 18.

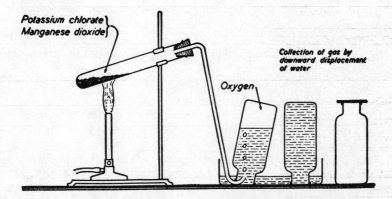

Fig. 18 — Lab. Preparation of Oxygen

3. COMMERCIAL PRODUCTION OF OXYGEN

(a) **From liquid air** — If air liquified by low temperature and high pressure is warmed, the nitrogen boils off (at $-196°C$) and leaves the oxygen whose boiling point is $-183°C$. This is the chief source.

(b) **By electrolysis of water** — Passage of an electric current through water decomposes it into hydrogen and oxygen ($2H_2O \longrightarrow 2H_2 + O_2$). A small amount of industrial oxygen is made this way.

4. FORMATION OF OXIDES

Many elements combine readily with oxygen forming oxides; the element is said to be oxidized; the reaction is an oxidation.

EXPERIMENT – Formation of some oxides
Method –

(i) Ignite a sample of each element in a deflagrating spoon and lower into a gas bottle of oxygen

(ii) Add 10 ml. of distilled water containing a few drops of bromthymol solution and a piece of litmus paper, cover and shake.

Observations –

(i) In distilled water bromthymol is green and litmus purple.

(ii) Carbon (charcoal) – a black solid; glows brightly, and disappears leaving a small gray ash; litmus turns red; bromthymol yellow.

(iii) Phosphorus (yellow) – a yellowish waxy solid; yellow flame; white solid formed which dissolves in water; litmus turns red and bromthymol yellow.

(iv) Sulphur – a yellow solid; blue flame, choking odour, litmus turns red and bromthymol yellow.

(v) Sodium – a soft silvery metal which tarnishes quickly in air; yellow flame, white solid which dissolves in water; litmus and bromthymol both turn blue.

(vi) Magnesium – silvery metallic solid; blinding white light; white solid formed, which is not very soluble in water; litmus and bromthymol turn blue.

(vii) Iron (steel wool) – grey metallic solid; brilliant sparks; dark gray substance remains which does not dissolve; no effect on litmus or bromthymol.

Conclusions –

In each case an oxide is formed; if light and heat are produced the reaction may be called burning – when this begins the substance is said to ignite; burning where oxygen is involved is called combustion. Litmus and bromthymol are indicators – i.e. they indicate the acidic or basic nature of the solution. In acid solution litmus is red and bromthymol yellow; in basic solution litmus and bromthymol are both blue.

Carbon – $C + O_2 \longrightarrow CO_2$ + heat

Carbon dioxide is a colorless odorless gas, somewhat soluble in water.

Phosphorus – $4P + 5O_2 \longrightarrow 2P_2O_5$ + heat

Phosphorus (V) oxide is a white solid, soluble in water.

Sulphur – $S + O_2 \longrightarrow SO_2$ + heat

Sulphur dioxide is a colorless gas with a choking odour, quite soluble in water, (there may be a small amount of a white solid (SO_3) formed also).

Sodium — $4Na + O_2 \longrightarrow 2Na_2O + heat$
Sodium oxide is a white solid quite soluble in water.

Magnesium — $2Mg + O_2 \longrightarrow 2MgO + heat$
Magnesium oxide is a white solid slightly soluble in water.

Iron — $3Fe + 2O_2 \longrightarrow Fe_3O_4 + heat$
(Magnetic) iron oxide is a dark gray solid, insoluble in water.

When the oxide dissolves in water it reacts with water to form an acid or base —

$CO_2 + H_2O \longrightarrow H_2CO_3$ carbonic acid

$P_2O_5 + 3H_2O \longrightarrow 2H_3PO_4$ phosphoric acid

$SO_2 + H_2O \longrightarrow H_2SO_3$ sulphurous acid

$Na_2O + H_2O \longrightarrow 2NaOH$ sodium hydroxide (a base)

$MgO + H_2O \longrightarrow Mg(OH)_2$ magnesium hydroxide (a base)

The elements carbon, phosphorus and sulphur form acidic oxides and are classified as non-metals. Sodium and magnesium form basic oxides and are classified as metals. Iron oxide is insoluble in water but for other reasons iron is classified as a metal.

Metal properties — (Na, Mg, Fe, Ca, Cu, etc.)
    (i)   Good conductors of heat and electricity.
    (ii) Grayish metallic lustre (except Cu and Au), ductile, malleable.
    (iii) Form basic oxides (oxides react with water to form bases.
    (iv) React with non-metals.

Non-metal properties — (C, P, S, Cl, O, etc.)
    (i)   Poor conductors of heat and electricity (except C).
    (ii) Colours vary; soft; dull or shiny.
    (iii) Form acidic oxides (oxides react with water to form acids)
    (iv) React with metals.

Acid properties —
    (i)   Turn litmus red and bromthymol yellow.
    (ii) Taste sour.
    (iii) Release hydrogen ion (H^+) when dissolved in water.
    (iv) React with a base to produce a salt and water.

Base properties –
(i) Turn litmus blue and bromthymol blue.
(ii) Taste bitter and often feel slippery.
(iii) Release hydroxide ion (OH^-) when dissolved in water.
(iv) React with an acid to produce a salt and water.

    e.g. $2NaOH + H_2CO_3 \longrightarrow Na_2CO_3 + 2H_2O$

         base + acid $\longrightarrow$ salt + water

5. COMBUSTION OF CARBONACEOUS (CARBON CONTAINING) SUBSTANCES

Most fuels contain carbon and hydrogen.
  e.g. natural gas – mainly methane – CH_4
        Propane – C_3H_8
        Gasoline – hydrocarbon – C_xH_y
        Coal – carbon – C
        Alcohol – CH_3OH
        Paraffin – hydrocarbons – C_xH_y

During combustion the carbon is oxidized to CO_2 and the hydrogen to H_2O.

EXPERIMENT – Products of combustion of fuels
Method –
Using flames from bunsen burner (natural gas), candle (paraffin) and an alcohol lamp, perform the following –
    (i) Hold a cold (ice & water), dry beaker over flame; place a pinch of anhydrous copper sulphate on bottom of beaker.
    (ii) Rinse a beaker with limewater and invert over flame.

Observations –
    (i) In each case a colorless liquid condenses on bottom of beaker and anhydrous copper sulphate turns blue.
    (ii) In each case limewater turns milky.

Conclusions –
    (i) H_2O formed – anhydrous $CuSO_4 + H_2O$ gives a blue colour which is a test for water.
    (ii) CO_2 formed – turns limewater milky – a test for CO_2.

Oxidation of carbon and hydrogen are exothermic reactions – the energy released is the useful product in combustion of fuels.

6. ENERGY RELEASE FROM COMBUSTION

A combustible substance has a temperature at which it will ignite (begin to produce obvious light and heat and continue without additional energy being supplied) — this is its ignition (kindling) temperature. Usually it is necessary to provide energy to raise the substance to its ignition temperature — an increase in temperature of 10°C approximately doubles the rate of most reactions. Different substances release different amounts of energy during combustion; examples of heats of combustion in kilocalories per gram are —

propane (C_3H_8)	11.9
alcohol (CH_3OH)	5.4
charcoal (C)	7.9
methane (CH_4)	13.3

EXPERIMENT — To determine heat of combustion of candle material (paraffin)

Method —

In a suitable calorimeter burn a known weight of candle; measure temperature of surrounding water before and after; find weight of water.

Observations —

Rise in temperature of water = t C°

Weight of water = m kilograms

Loss in weight of candle = w grams

Conclusions —

Heat gained by water = mt kilocalories

Heat of combustion of paraffin = $\dfrac{mt}{w}$ kilocalories per gram.

7. LOW TEMPERATURE OXIDATIONS

Oxidation of many substances takes place at room temperature at rates which are noticeable —

e.g. Iron rusts $4Fe + 3O_2 \longrightarrow 2Fe_2O_3$(rust) + heat

Sodium tarnishes $4Na + O_2 \longrightarrow 2Na_2O$ + heat

White Phosphorus fumes $4P + 5O_2 \longrightarrow 2P_2O_5$ + heat

Spontaneous combustion (self ignition) is brought about by slow oxidation at room temperature raising the temperature of the substance to its ignition temperature. This may occur if the heat released does not escape to the surroundings rapidly enough — oily rags, coal piles, damp hay, etc.

EXPERIMENT – To show spontaneous combustion
Method –
Dissolve a pea-sized piece of white phosphorus in 5 ml. of CS_2.
Pour solution over filter paper in fume hood.

Observations –
White smoke (fumes); filter paper ignites

Conclusions –
Oxidation of P at room temperature raises it to its ignition temp-
ature – this in turn ignites the paper.
When exposed to moist air some metals form a thin tightly ad-
hering layer of oxidation product which protects the underlying
metal from corrosion –
    e.g. Aluminium forms Al_2O_3 – a dull oxide coating
        Copper forms $Cu(OH)_2$. $CuCO_3$ – a green basic carbonate

EXPERIMENT – Removal of protective coating on aluminium
Dip a piece of aluminium in H_2O and in dilute HCl – no reaction
with water and a very slow reaction with HCl. Clean aluminium
with steel wool and dip in $HgCl_2$ solution for a few seconds –
then dip in H_2O or in dilute HCl; it now displaces hydrogen from
H_2O or from dilute HCl. Aluminium is high in the activity series
of metals but does not react readily until the oxide layer is
removed by reaction with $HgCl_2$.

8. IMPORTANCE OF OXYGEN
(a) In respiration – in every living cell food is oxidized to
release energy for heat, movement, growth, etc.

$$C_6H_{12}O_6(sugar) + 6O_2 \longrightarrow 6CO_2 + 6H_2O + energy$$

(b) In oxidation of fuels to release heat energy in the home
and in industry.

(c) In medical treatment where lung action is diminished –
oxygen tent (40%-60% oxygen) and oxygen masks (firemen etc).

(d) To increase rate of combustion for more rapid energy release
in rockets, high temperature in oxy-acetylene torch, or more
quickly attaining a high temperature in the blast furnace (steel
making).

UNIT VII: HYDROGEN

I. NATURAL OCCURRENCE
In the atmosphere of the sun and other stars. Small quantities in volcanic and natural gases. Combined in H_2O, organic compounds, rocks and minerals.

2. LABORATORY PREPARATION
(a) EXPERIMENT — Action of H_2O on active metals
Method —
    (i)   Place small ($\frac{1}{8}$") cubes of Na and K on water.

    (ii) Wrap small cubes of Na and K in lead foil and place in water; trap gas evolved in water filled test tubes.

    (iii) Add Ca to water; collect gas evolved.

    (iv) Bring burning splint to mouth of test tubes filled with gas from (ii) and (iii); also test tubes containing mixtures of this gas with air.

    (v) Add litmus and bromthymol to water from (ii) and (iii).

Observations —
Na is a silvery metallic solid; floats, melts, disappears.
K is a bluish silvery metallic solid, floats, melts, ignites, mauve flame, disappears.
Ca is a grey metallic solid, sinks, colorless gas evolved, water becomes milky.
Litmus turns blue; bromthymol blue.
Gas in full test tube burns with a blue flame.
Gas and air mixture explodes.

Conclusions —
These active metals react with H_2O releasing hydrogen (a colorless gas).

$$2Na + 2H_2O \longrightarrow H_2 \uparrow + 2NaOH$$
$$2K + 2H_2O \longrightarrow H_2 \uparrow + 2KOH$$
$$Ca + 2H_2O \longrightarrow H_2 \uparrow + Ca(OH)_2$$

The hydroxides formed are bases (turn litmus blue); NaOH and KOH are quite soluble in water but $Ca(OH)_2$ is only slightly soluble. Hydrogen burns quietly when pure but is very explosive when mixed with air.

$$2H_2 + O_2 \longrightarrow 2H_2O + heat$$

(b) EXPERIMENT – Reaction of less active metals with H₂O (steam)

Method –
(i) Lower burning magnesium into a flask of steam.
(ii) Pass steam over hot iron – Fig. 19.

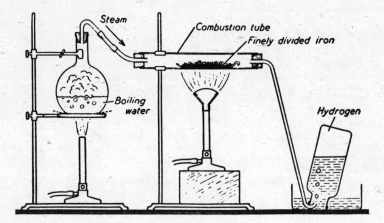

Fig. 19 – Reduction of steam by iron

(iii) Pass steam over heated copper as in Fig. 19.

Observations and Conclusions –

(i) Magnesium continues to burn; a white solid is formed. Magnesium (burning) reacts with steam –

$Mg + H_2O \longrightarrow MgO + H_2 \uparrow$ (hydrogen which is formed burns)

(ii) A colorless gas is collected which burns; iron turns dark gray. Hot iron reacts with steam –

$$3Fe + 4H_2O \longrightarrow Fe_3O_4 + 4H_2 \uparrow$$

(iii) No change in copper; copper is not active enough to react with steam.

(c) EXPERIMENT – Reaction of dilute acids with metals
Method –

Add pieces of (i) Mg and (ii) Fe and (iii) Cu to dilute HCl and H₂SO₄. Test any gas evolved, with a burning splint.

Observations –

Observations are the same with HCl and H_2SO_4.

    (i)   Mg reacts vigorously; colorless gas formed burns.

    (ii) Fe reaction slower than in (i); colorless gas burns.

    (iii) Cu has no reaction.

Conclusions –

Mg and Fe displace H_2 from dilute acids but Cu has no reaction.

$$Mg + 2HCl \longrightarrow H_2 \uparrow + MgCl_2$$

$$Fe + H_2SO_4 \longrightarrow H_2 \uparrow + FeSO_4$$

3. COMMERCIAL PRODUCTION

Three methods –

    (i)   Cracking of natural gas (mostly CH_4) by high temperature.

$$CH_4 \xrightarrow{\text{1000°C}} 2H_2 + C$$

    (ii) Steam is forced over white hot coke (carbon).

$$C + H_2O \longrightarrow CO + H_2$$

The mixture of CO and H_2 is water gas; if pure H_2 is wanted the CO may be removed by oxidizing it, with more steam and a catalyst, to form CO_2 which is removed by passing it through a basic solution.

    (iii) Electrolysis of water in areas where electricity is cheap.

$$2H_2O \longrightarrow 2H_2 + O_2$$

Hydrogen has many uses in industry.

4. CHEMICAL PROPERTIES OF HYDROGEN

(a) With oxygen

    EXPERIMENT – The burning of hydrogen

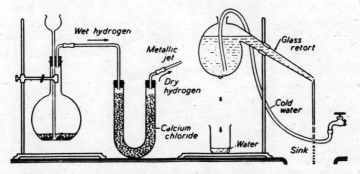

Fig. 20 – Burning hydrogen

Method –
See Fig. 20. The hydrogen must not be ignited until test tubes of the gas collected at the jet burn quietly. Test liquid, condensed on retort, with anhydrous copper sulphate.

Observations –
Hydrogen burns at the jet with a pale blue flame; the colorless liquid formed turns anhydrous copper sulphate blue.

Conclusions –
$$2H_2 + O_2 \longrightarrow 2H_2O$$
Pure hydrogen burns quietly. Hydrogen mixed with air (or oxygen) forms an explosive mixture over a wide range of concentrations – (approximately 6% to 70% hydrogen).
Other fuel gases form explosive mixtures with air –

e.g. Gasoline vapour   1.5 – 6.0%
      Propane   2.5 – 10%
      Methane (natural gas)   6.0 – 13%

(b) With metal oxides
Hydrogen will reduce some metal oxides.

     EXPERIMENT – Reaction of H$_2$ with hot CuO (copper (II) oxide)

     Method – Fig. 21

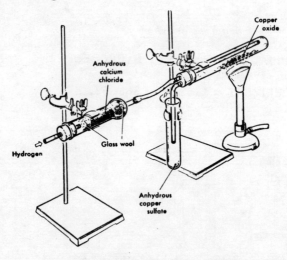

Fig. 21 – Reduction of CuO by H$_2$

Observations —

Black CuO becomes copper colored. Anhydrous copper sulphate turns blue.

Conclusions —

CuO has been reduced to Cu; H_2 has been oxidized to H_2O.

$$CuO + H_2 \longrightarrow H_2O + Cu$$

EXPERIMENT — Reaction of H_2 on hot Fe_3O_4

In Unit VII 2(b) (ii) it was shown that steam will react with hot iron to produce magnetic iron oxide and hydrogen. If however H_2 is passed over Fe_3O_4 at a higher temperature the reaction is reversed. These two processes constitute a reversible reaction —

$$3Fe + 4H_2O \rightleftharpoons Fe_3O_4 + 4H_2$$

The direction depends on conditions — a higher temperature and an excess of hydrogen tend to make the reaction go to the left.

5. ACTIVITIES OF METALS

The activity series is a list of metals arranged in order of decreasing activity in respect to various reactions —

for example: (i) vigour of reaction with oxygen

(ii) ability to displace hydrogen from water or dilute acids

Hydrogen is included in the series, and placed just below those metals which will displace it. This series includes (most active first) — K, Na, Ca, Mg, Al, Zn, Fe, H, Cu, Hg, Ag. The more active the metal the more readily it gives up an electron(s) to become an ion.

UNIT VIII: ATOMIC WEIGHTS, MOLECULAR WEIGHTS AND MOLES

1. Atomic weight and mass number were defined in Unit II. Masses of atoms and molecules may be compared by the mass spectrograph – Fig. 22.

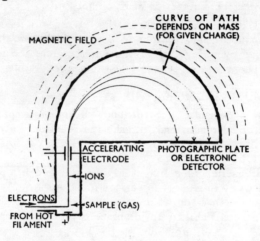

Fig. 22 – The Mass Spectrograph

In this instrument gas particles are ionized by electron bombardment then directed across a magnetic field; the paths of heavy particles are bent less than those of lighter particles and their relative masses can be found by calculation.

2. Molecular weights

Some substances consist of molecules (Unit III). The weights of molecules in atomic mass units (a.m.u.) are called molecular weights; an atomic mass unit is $\frac{1}{12}$ of the mass of an atom of $_6C^{12}$ (1.66×10^{-24} g.). A molecular weight can be found by adding the atomic weights in the molecular formula.

e.g. water (H_2O) – molecular weight = $(2 \times 1) + 16 = 18$ (a.m.u.)

or chloroform ($CHCl_3$) – molecular weight = $12 + 1 + (3 \times 35.5)$
$$= 119.5 \text{ (a.m.u.)}$$

Molecular weights give relative weights of molecules.

e.g. $\dfrac{\text{wt of water molecule}}{\text{wt of chloroform molecule}} = \dfrac{18\ \text{a.m.u.}}{119.5\ \text{a.m.u.}} = \dfrac{1}{6.6}$

i.e. a chloroform molecule is 6.6 times as heavy as a water molecule.

The molecular weight expressed in grams is the gram-molecular weight.

In an ionic substance the sum of the atomic weights in the simplest unit is the formula weight.

e.g. sodium sulphate (Na_2SO_4 is the simplest unit)

formula weight = $(2 \times 23) + (1 \times 32) + (4 \times 16) = 142$ (a.m.u.)

In using atomic weights, molecule weights and formula weights, the unit (a.m.u.) is usually omitted.

3. THE MOLE

It has been found from experiment that the number of atoms in the gram atomic weight of an element or the number of molecules in a gram molecular weight of an element or compound is always the same – this number, called A v o g a d r o 's N u m b e r (N) is 6.02×10^{23}.

This number of atoms or molecules is called a mole. 1 mole may refer to any of the following –

    (i)   1 gram – molecular weight

    (ii) 6.02×10^{23} atoms of an element

    (iii) 6.02×10^{23} molecules of a molecular substance

    (iv) 1 gram – formula weight

The gram – atomic weight may now be defined as the weight in grams of 1 mole of atoms (N atoms) of the element and the gram-molecular weight as the weight in grams of N molecules of the molecular substance (element or compound).

4. AVOGADRO'S PRINCIPLE

Equal volumes of gases, measured at the same temperature and pressure, contain equal numbers of molecules.

This was first suggested by Avogadro (1811) from observations that gases always combine in simple whole number ratios.

5. GRAM-MOLECULAR (MOLAR) VOLUME (OF A GAS)

This is the volume occupied by 1 mole of any gas. At S.T.P. (0°C and 760 mm. pressure) it is 22.4 litres.

6. FINDING GRAM-MOLECULAR WEIGHTS

(a) **From molecular formula** — (Unit VIII 2)

(b) **From gas density** — If the weight of a known volume of a gaseous element or compound, at known temperature and pressure, is found, the weight of 22.4 litres at S.T.P. (1 mole) can be calculated. e.g. 1.33 litres of a gas at 91°C and 380 mm. pressure weigh 0.625 g. Find its gram-molecular weight.

Solution —

Volume at S.T.P. $= 1.33 \; 1 \times \dfrac{380 \text{ mm}}{760 \text{ mm}} \times \dfrac{273°K}{364°K} = 0.50 \; 1.$

∴ 0.50 l. at S.T.P. weigh 0.625 g.

∴ 22.4 l. at S.T.P. weigh $\dfrac{22.4}{0.50} \times 0.625$ g. = 28.0 g.

∴ Gram-molecular weight = 28.0 g.

7. PROBLEMS

(a) **Percentage composition by weight from formula** —

e.g. Magnesium oxide (MgO)

Formula weight = 24.3 + 16.0 = 40.3

Magnesium $= \dfrac{24.3}{40.3} \times 100 = 60.3\%$

Oxygen $= \dfrac{16.0}{40.3} \times 100 = 39.7\%$

(b) **Simplest formula from composition by weight**

Problem — a compound of carbon and oxygen is 27.3% carbon; find its simplest formula.

Solution —

Elements	Ratio by Weights	Ratio of Atoms	Ratio of Atoms in Whole Numbers	Formula
Carbon	27.3 g.	$\dfrac{27.3}{12} = 2.27$	1	CO_2
Oxygen	72.7 g.	$\dfrac{72.7}{16} = 4.54$	2	

(c) Molecular formula from simplest formula and molecular weight.

Problem — A compound (ethane) has a simplest formula CH_3 and a molecular weight of 30.0. Find its molecular formula.

Solution — Formula weight of CH_3 = 12.0 + (3 × 1.0) = 15.0

∴ the number of CH_3 units in the molecular formula

must be $\dfrac{30.0}{15.0}$ = 2

∴ the molecular formula is C_2H_6

(d) Number of atoms

Problem — Find the number of atoms of oxygen in 10 grams of glucose sugar ($C_6H_{12}O_6$).

Solution

Molecular weight of glucose = $(6 \times 12.0) + (12 \times 1.0) + (6 \times 16.0) = 180$

180 grams glucose contain 6.02×10^{23} molecules

∴ 10 grams glucose contain $\dfrac{10}{180} \times 6.02 \times 10^{23}$

$$= 3.34 \times 10^{22} \text{ molecules.}$$

1 molecule of glucose contains 6 atoms of oxygen

∴ 3.34×10^{22} molecules of glucose contain

$6 \times 3.34 \times 10^{22}$

$= 2.00 \times 10^{23}$ atoms of oxygen.

(e) Gram - molecular weight of a gas — see Unit VIII 6.

(f) Mass, volume, temperature and pressure relationships of gases of known molecular weight.

For the 4 problems following, the gas is carbon dioxide CO_2 — molecular weight 44.0.

Problem (i) — Find the mass of 5.0 litres of CO_2 at a pressure of 380 mm and a temperature of 91°C.

Solution —

Volume at S.T.P. = $5.0 \text{ l.} \times \dfrac{380}{760} \times \dfrac{273}{364}$ = 1.9 litres

22.4 litres at S.T.P. weigh 44.0 g.

∴ 1.9 l. at S.T.P. weigh $\dfrac{1.9}{22.4} \times 44.0$ g. = 3.7 g.

Problem (ii) — Find the volume of 2.0 grams of CO_2 at 2.0 atmospheres pressure and a temperature of $182°C$.

Solution —

44.0 g. of CO_2 at S.T.P. occupy 22.4 l.

$\therefore$ 2.0 g. CO_2 at S.T.P. occupy $\dfrac{2.0}{44.0} \times 22.4$ l. = 1.02 l.

Volume at 2 atmospheres pressure and $182°C$. =

1.02 l. $\times \dfrac{455}{273} \times \dfrac{1}{2}$ = 0.85 l.

Problem (iii) — Find the temperature at which 10.0 g. of CO_2 has a volume of 15.0 litres at a pressure of 0.25 atmospheres.

Solution

44.0 g. CO_2 has a volume of 22.4 l. at S.T.P.

$\therefore$ 10.0 g. at S.T.P. has a volume of $\dfrac{10.0}{44.0} \times 22.4$ l. = 5.1 l.

Let the temperature to be found = $T°K$

$\therefore$ 5.1 l. $\times \dfrac{1}{0.25} \times \dfrac{T}{273}$ = 15.0 l.

$\therefore T = \dfrac{15}{5.1} \times \dfrac{0.25}{1} \times 273$ = 200

$\therefore$ Temperature = $200°K$. or $-73°C$.

Problem (iv) — Find the pressure at which 8.0 g. CO_2 at $273°C$ occupies 3000 ml.

Solution —

8.0 g. CO_2 at S.T.P. occupies $\dfrac{8.0}{44.0} \times 22.4$ l. = 4.1 l.

Let the pressure to be found be P mm. of mercury.

$\therefore$ 4.1 l. $\times \dfrac{546}{273} \times \dfrac{760}{P}$ = 3.0 l.

$\therefore P = \dfrac{4.1}{3.0} \times \dfrac{546}{273} \times 760$ mm. = 2052 mm.

$\therefore$ the required pressure = 2052 mm. or 2.7 atmospheres.

(g) Concentration of molecules in a gas —

Problem — A volume of 2.0 litres of oxygen at a certain temperature and pressure weighs 3.2 grams. Find the concentration of molecules in this gas - (number of molecules per millilitre).

Solution —

1 mole of oxygen (32 g.) contains 6.02×10^{23} molecules.

$\therefore$ 3.2 grams Oxygen contain $\frac{3.2}{32} \times 6.02 \times 10^{23}$ molecules $=$

6.02×10^{22} molecules.

$\therefore$ 2.0 l. contains 6.02×10^{22} molecules.

$\therefore$ 1 ml. contains $\frac{6.02 \times 10^{22}}{2000} = 3.01 \times 10^{19}$ molecules.

8. EXPERIMENTS

(a) Experiment to find the molar volume of oxygen at S.T.P.

Method —

(i) Make a gas bag as follows; insert a medicine dropper into the small end of a large one-hole stopper; with a rubberband fix this stopper in the open end of a plastic bag of about 1 quart volume.

(ii) Press air out of bag and weigh to 0.01 g. (W_1 g.)

(iii) Fill bag with oxygen at room temperature and pressure and weigh again. (W_2 g.)

(iv) Expel oxygen into a large bottle of water inverted in water; measure volume of water needed to fill bottle again — this gives volume of oxygen weighed — (V litres).

(v) Record room temperature and pressure. (t^0C. and p. mm.)

(vi) Look up density of air at t^0C. and p. mm. pressure.

Calculation —

Apparent weight of oxygen $= W_2$ g. $- W_1$ g. $= W_3$ g.

Find buoyant force of air on bag of oxygen (weight of V litres of air at t^0C. and p. mm. $= W_4$ g.)

$\therefore$ Weight of oxygen $= W_3$ g. $+ W_4$ g. $= W_5$ g.

$\therefore$ V litres of oxygen at t^0C. and p. mm. pressure weigh W_5 g.

Calculate the volume at S.T.P. of 32 g. (1 mole) of oxygen. This should be 22.4 litres within experimental error.

(b) Experiment — To find the ratio by weight of equal volumes of different gases.

Method —

Using the apparatus and method of Exp. (a) find the weights of a bag full of oxygen and a bag full of carbon dioxide (equal volumes.)

Calculation —

Find the ratio $\frac{\text{weight of } CO_2}{\text{weight of } O_2}$ this should be equal to 1.38 (same as mole ratio $\frac{44}{32}$).

(c) Experiment — Finding formula of mercury (II) oxide.

In Unit I experiment (c) the percentage composition of mercury (II) oxide was found. Using the method of unit VIII 7 (b), use this percentage composition to find its formula (HgO).

(d) Experiment — To find the number of moles of silver displaced by 1 mole of copper —

Method —
   (i)   Dissolve a weighed sample of $AgNO_3$ in water.
   (ii) Immerse in the solution a weighed coil of copper wire and leave for 24 hours.
   (iii) Using a wash bottle rinse copper coil into $AgNO_3$ solution.
   (iv) Dry copper coil and weigh.
   (v) Decant $AgNO_3$ solution and wash residue (crystals) several times.
   (vi) Dry residue and weigh.

Observations —
Silver crystals form in $AgNO_3$ solution; solution turns blue.

Conclusions —
Loss in weight of copper = W_1 g.
Weight of silver crystals = W_2 g.
Copper goes into solution as Cu^{2+} ion which is blue.
Silver is displaced forming crystals.

$$Cu + 2AgNO_3 \longrightarrow Cu(NO_3)_2 + 2Ag$$

Number of moles of Cu used = $\dfrac{W_1}{63.5}$ = a

Number of moles of Ag displaced = $\dfrac{W_2}{108}$ = b

From the equation 1 mole of Cu produces 2 moles of Ag

$\therefore$ The ratio $\dfrac{b}{a}$ should be 2 (within experimental error).

(e) Experiment — To find the number of moles of H_2 produced by 1 mole of Mg.

Method — see Fig. 23.
   (i)   Coil and weigh a piece of magnesium ribbon about 8" long.
   (ii) Fill a 200 ml. gas measuring tube with 10% Hcl.
   (iii) Invert the tube in water and push into it the coil of magnesium.

(iv) When the reaction is over, cool the tube to temperature of water; record volume of gas collected.

(v) Record temperature of water and atmospheric pressure.

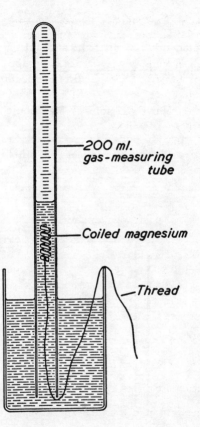

Fig. 23 – Displacement of H₂ by Mg.

Observations – (a possible set of measurements)
A colorless gas is produced; magnesium disappears.
   Volume of gas   = 150 ml.
   Weight of Mg   = 0.142 g.
Temperature = 22°C.   Pressure = 750 mm.

Calculations — Mg + 2Hcl. $\longrightarrow$ H$_2$ + MgCl$_2$

Apparent pressure of hydrogen produced = 750 mm.

Actual pressure = 750 mm. − 20 mm. (vapour pressure of H$_2$O at 22°C.)

∴ Vol. of H$_2$ at S.T.P. = 150 ml. × $\dfrac{730}{760}$ × $\dfrac{273}{295}$ = 133 ml.

∴ 0.142 g. Mg. produces 133 ml. of H$_2$ at S.T.P.

∴ 24.3 g. (1 mole) of Mg produces $\dfrac{24.3}{0.142}$ × $\dfrac{133}{22400}$ moles = 1.02

moles of H$_2$[8]

From the equation above, 1 mole of Mg should give 1 mole of hydrogen (2% error).

(f) Experiment — Ratio by volume in which hydrogen and oxygen write.

Method — See Fig. 24.

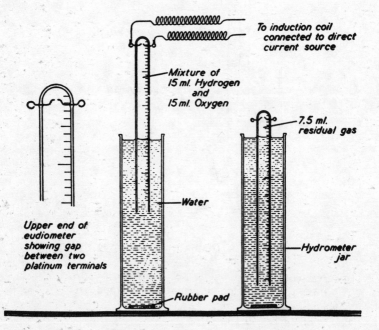

Fig. 24 — Reaction between Oxygen and Hydrogen

(i)   Pass 15 ml. of H_2 and 15 ml. O_2 into a 50 ml. eudiometer tube.

(ii) Place heavy plastic screen between eudiometer and observers — (eudiometer may shatter).

(iii) Hold eudiometer with towel and pass spark through gas mixture.

(iv) Cool and measure volume of residual gas.

(v)   Test residual gas with splint.

Observations —

Volume of residual gas = 7.5 ml. Glowing splint ignites in residual gas.

Conclusions —

Residual gas is O_2

Volume of H_2 used = 15 ml.

Volume of O_2 used = 7.5 ml.

$$2H_2 + O_2 \longrightarrow 2H_2O$$

H_2O condenses to a liquid on cooling.

$$\frac{\text{Vol. of } H_2}{\text{Vol. of } O_2} = \frac{15 \text{ ml.}}{7.5 \text{ ml.}} = \frac{2}{1} \quad \text{(Gases at same t and p).}$$

UNIT IX: CALCULATIONS FROM EQUATIONS

A balanced equation may be used to solve problems concerning quantitative relationships in a reaction; these quantities may involve weights, volumes or moles.

Since an equation connects quantities of reactants and products in mole units, it is best to get the desired information from the equation in moles, and then convert if necessary to the desired units.

I. WEIGHT – WEIGHT RELATIONSHIPS –

Problem – Find the weight of $Ca(OH)_2$ produced from 10 g. of Calcium reacting with excess water.

Balanced equation is $Ca + 2H_2O \longrightarrow H_2 + Ca(OH)_2$

Solution –

10 g. Calcium is $\dfrac{10}{40}$ moles $= 0.25$ moles.

From equation 1 mole of Ca produces 1 mole of $Ca(OH)_2$

$\therefore$ 0.25 moles of Ca produce 0.25 moles of $Ca(OH)_2$

1 mole of $Ca(OH)_2$ $= 74$ g.

$\therefore$ weight of $Ca(OH)_2$ $= 0.25 \times 74$ g. $= 18.5$ g.

2. WEIGHT – VOLUME RELATIONSHIPS –

Problem – Find the weight of Ca needed to produce, by reaction with water, 11.2 litres of H_2 at -91^0C. and 2 atmospheres pressure.

Solution –

$Ca + 2H_2O \longrightarrow H_2 + Ca(OH)_2$

1 mole of H_2 is 22.4 l. at S.T.P.

Vol. of H_2 required, at S.T.P. $= 11.2$ l. $\times \dfrac{273}{182} \times \dfrac{2}{1} = 33.6$ l.

33.6 l. at S.T.P. $= \dfrac{33.6}{22.4}$ moles $= 1.5$ moles.

1 mole of H_2 is produced by 1 mole of Ca.

$\therefore$ 1.5 moles of H_2 are produced by 1.5 moles of Ca.

1.5 moles of Ca $= 1.5 \times 40$ g. $= 60$ g.

$\therefore$ 60 g. calcium are needed.

3. VOLUME — VOLUME RELATIONSHIPS —

Problem — Find the volume of O_2 needed to burn 5 l. of propane (C_3H_8) — both gases at same t and p.

Solution —

$$C_3H_8 + 5O_2 \longrightarrow 3CO_2 + 4H_2O$$

1 mole of propane needs 5 moles of oxygen.

1 mole of O_2 occupies same volume as 1 mole of C_3H_8 at same temperature and pressure.

$\therefore$ 1 volume of C_3H_8 need 5 volumes of O_2

$\therefore$ 5 litres of C_3H_8 needs 25 litres of O_2 at same temperature and pressure.

UNIT X: WATER AND SOLUTIONS

I. WATER —

(a) Occurrence and importance —
70% of earth's surface to an average depth of 2 miles; 100,000 tons of water vapour over every sq. mile of earth's surface; 65% of the human body.

Water is essential to plant and animal life (solvent for reactions, transportation systems etc). Natural water is never pure. A cubic mile of sea water contains over 150 million tons of dissolved compounds — it is a source of sodium chloride, bromine, magnesium etc.

(b) Physical Properties —
Freezing point = 0^oC. at 760 mm. pressure

Boiling point = 100^oC. at 760 mm. pressure - rises as pressure increases.

Vapour pressure — see Unit IV 2 (e)

Density = 1 gram per ml. at 0^oC.; increases as temperature decreases to 4^oC. where it is a maximum — then decreases to the freezing point; on freezing, density decreases so that it floats on water (expansion on freezing is approx. 9%).

(c) Standards for measurement — many are based on water —
1 litre (l.) = the volume of 1 kilogram of water at 4^oC. (maximum density)

1 calorie = the amount of heat needed to raise the temperature of 1 gram of water 1 C.^{o}.

Specific gravity = the ratio of the density of a substance to the density of water.

Temperature — the freezing and boiling points of water are used as fixed points on Centigrade and Fahrenheit temperature scales.

(d) Composition —
(i) In Unit VIII 8 (f) the ratio by volume in which hydrogen and oxygen unite to form water was found to be 2:1. This volume ratio can be found also by decomposing water by an electric current (electrolysis) as in Fig. 25.

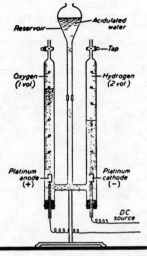

Fig. 25 — Electrolysis of Water

Here the volumes of gases produced can be measured and the gases tested (O_2 ignites a glowing splint; hydrogen burns).

(ii) The composition of water by weight can be found from the reduction of CuO by H_2 (Unit VII 4 (b)) by using the modification in apparatus shown in Fig. 26.

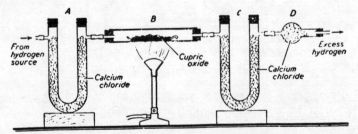

Fig. 26 — Finding Composition of Water by weight.

Weight of water formed = gain in weight of tube C = a grams
Weight of oxygen used = loss in weight of tube B = b grams
∴ Weight of hydrogen used = (a – b) grams = c grams.

∴ % by weight of oxygen in water = $\dfrac{b}{a} \times 100$ = 89% (approx.)

% by weight hydrogen in water = $\dfrac{c}{a} \times 100$ = 11% (approx.)

2. HYDRATES –

A hydrate is a substance formed when a salt crystallizes from solution combined loosely with a definite amount of water; this water is called water of hydration or water of crystallization.

(a) Experiment – To study heating of a hydrate

Method –

(i) Heat bluestone crystals (copper (II) sulphate penta-hydrate) as in Fig. 27 until no further change.

(ii) Add a drop of water to solid left in test tube.

(iii) Add a drop of liquid from vertical test tube to some anhydrous copper sulphate.

Bluestone crystals

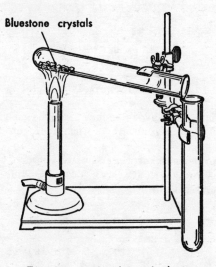

Fig. 27 – Heating a hydrate.

Observations – Colorless liquid collects in test tube, which turns anhydrous copper sulphate blue. Bluestone turns to a crumbly white solid which turns blue when water is added to it.

Conclusions – Bluestone is a hydrate; water is driven off quite easily on heating leaving anhydrous copper sulphate. (test for water – turns anhydrous copper sulphate blue).

$$CuSO_4 \cdot 5H_2O \underset{\text{Low temp.}}{\overset{\text{High temp.}}{\rightleftharpoons}} CuSO_4 + 5H_2O$$

(b) Experiment — To find the composition of a hydrate.
Method —
   (i)   Weigh a clean dry test tube (W_1 grams).
   (ii)   Add some barium chloride dihydrate crystals and weigh again (W_2 grams).
   (iii) Arrange test tube horizontally and heat until no more water is being released.
   (iv) Cool and weigh again (W_3 grams).

Calculations —
Weight of crystals = $(W_2 - W_1)$ grams
Weight of water given off = $(W_2 - W_3)$ grams

$$\therefore \text{ \% water is crystals } = \frac{W_2 - W_3}{W_2 - W_1} \times 100\%$$

From the formula $BaCl_2 \cdot 2H_2O$, 1 mole = 244 g.
1 mole contains 36 g. water.

$$\therefore \text{ \% water } = \frac{36}{244} \times 100 = 14.7\% \text{ (this should agree with the}$$

calculation above).

(c) Efflorescence —
Some hydrates hold their water of hydration so loosely that it can be given off into the air at room temperature; this process is efflorescence.
Washing soda crystals (Na_2CO_3 $10H_2O$) soon crumble to powder when exposed to air; bluestone ($CuSO_4 \cdot 5H_2O$) turns white slowly in dry air.

(d) Hygroscopic and Deliquescent Substances —
Some substances attract water molecules from the air to become hydrates — such a substance is said to be hygroscopic; if the absorption of water continues until the substance dissolves, it is said to be deliquescent (the process is deliquescence).
   eg. $CaCl_2 + 6H_2O \longrightarrow CaCl_2 \cdot 6H_2O$
If left exposed to air the calcium chloride will dissolve to form a liquid solution. An anhydrous deliquescent substance (eg. $CaCl_2$) is often used as a dehydrating agent.

Problem — A substance is known to be a hydrate of calcium sulphate and is found to be 20.9% water. Find its formula.

Solution —

Substances	Ratio in grams	Ratio in moles	Whole number ratio
$CaSO_4$	79.1	$\dfrac{79.1}{136} = 0.58$	1
H_2O	20.9	$\dfrac{20.9}{18} = 1.16$	2

$\therefore$ Formula is $CaSO_4 \cdot 2H_2O$ (gypsum.)

3. SOLUTIONS —

A solution consists of two or more substances; the one which occurs to the greater extent is the solvent, the other (or others) is the solute.

(a) Characteristics —

(i) Homogeneous (one phase) — a phase is a form of matter consisting of similar parts, separated from other forms by definite boundaries - (eg. ice and water in a glass are 2 phases but one substance).

(ii) Constituents do not settle out (eg. sugar does not settle out from a solution of sugar in water).

(iii) Composition variable within limits. (eg. sugar will dissolve in water to form a solution up to a certain concentration - but no more). Some substances will form solutions in all proportions - (eg. alcohol and water) - such substances are said to be miscible.

(b) Solubility — May be defined as the maximum amount of solute which will dissolve in a certain quantity of solvent, which is in contact with excess solute, at a given temperature.

Solubilities are usually expressed in grams of solute per 100 grams of solvent. In Fig. 28 solubilities of several salts in water at different temperatures are given.

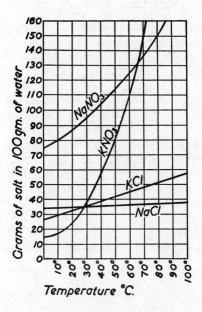

Fig. 28 — Solubility curves

(c) Types of Solutions —
Solids, liquids, or gases may be solvents or solutes.

Solvent	Solute	Example
solid	solid	brass (zinc in copper)
solid	liquid	amalgam (mercury in gold)
solid	gas	hydrogen in palladium
liquid	solid	sugar in water
liquid	liquid	alcohol in water
liquid	gas	soda water (CO_2 in water)
gas	gas	air (oxygen in nitrogen)

(d) Concentration of Solutions —
Several methods are used for expressing concentration —

   (i)   Percentage by weight (weight-percent) — here the amount of solute is expressed as a percentage of the weight of the solution.

   (ii)   Weight of solute per 100 grams of solvent — this is the method usually used for solubilities — Fig. 28.

(iii) Weight of solute per litre of solution — (grams per litre — g.p.l.)

(iv) Molarity — number of moles of solute per litre of solution (M).

Problem — A solution is made by dissolving 43 grams of common salt (NaCl) in 325 ml. of water — the volume of the solution is 330 ml.

Express the concentration of the solution as —

    (i)   Percentage by weight.

    (ii)   Weight of solute per 100 grams of solvent

    (iii) Weight of solute per litre of solution.

    (iv) Molarity.

Solution —

    (i)   Weight of solution is 43 g. + 325 g. = 368 g.

$$\text{\% by weight of solute} = \frac{43}{368} \times 100 = 11.7\%$$

    (ii)   325 g. (325 ml.) of solvent (water) contains 43 grams of solute (salt).

$$\therefore \text{100 g. solvent contains } \frac{100}{325} \times 43 \text{ g.} = 13.2 \text{ g. salt.}$$

    (iii) 330 ml. of solution contains 43 g. salt.

$$\therefore \text{1 l. of solution contains } \frac{1000}{330} \times 43 \text{ g.} = 130.3 \text{ g. salt.}$$

    (iv) 1 mole of NaCl = 58.5 g.

1 litre of solution contains 130.3 g. salt (iii)

$$\therefore \text{1 l. of solution contains } \frac{130.3}{58.5} \text{ moles} = 2.2 \text{ moles of salt.}$$

∴ Solution is 2.2 M.

UNIT XI: IONS IN AQUEOUS SOLUTION

I. CONDUCTION OF ELECTRICITY –
(a) In metals by free movement of electrons from atom to atom.

(b) In aqueous solution by movement of charged ions. An electrolyte is a substance whose solution in water will conduct an electric current – eg. NaCl. A non-electrolyte is a substance whose solution in water will not conduct an electric current – eg. sugar.

2. SOURCE OF IONS –
(a) Dissociation of ions of an electrovalent (ionic) compound when melted or dissolved in water.
eg. $Na^+Cl^- \longrightarrow Na^+ + Cl^-$

(b) Reaction of a covalent compound with water –
eg. $HCl + H_2O \longrightarrow H_3O^+ + Cl^-$
This process is ionization. H_3O^+ (or $H^+ \cdot H_2O$) is called the hydronium ion or hydrated hydrogen ion – for simplicity it is usually written H^+ and called the hydrogen ion.

Avogadro's number (N) of ions is called 1 mole of ions.

3. ELECTROLYSIS –
is the chemical change produced in the solution of an electrolyte by the passage of an electric current. The meanings of electrode, anode, and cathode are explained by Fig. 29.

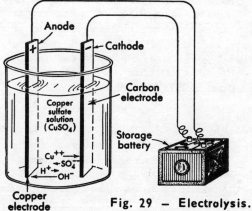

Fig. 29 – Electrolysis.

(a) Experiment —

To compare conductivities of aqueous solutions.

Method — Fig. 30.

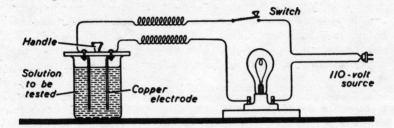

Fig. 30 — Conductivity of Solutions.

Place solution in the cell, close switch and observe brightness of light.

Observations — A bright light was observed with HCl, NaCl, or NaOH in water. No light with CH_3OH (methanol) or $C_{12}H_{22}O_{11}$ (sucrose) in water or HCl in carbon tetrachloride.

Conclusions — HCl, NaCl, and NaOH are electrolytes, — in water they form ions by dissociation or ionization. Water is an ionizing solvent (it encourages the formation of ions). Methanol and sucrose are non-electrolytes. A substance (eg. HCl) may form ions in one solvent (water) but not in another solvent (CCl_4).

(b) Experiment — **To study electrolysis of various substances.**

Method — Pass an electric current through the following solutions as illustrated in Fig. 29.

Observations —

(i)   Hydrochloric acid — at cathode a colorless gas which is explosive when mixed with air; at anode a slightly greenish gas which has a chlorine odour and bleaches litmus.

(ii)   Copper (II) sulphate — at cathode a brown solid deposit; at anode a colorless gas which ignites a glowing splint.

(iii) Sodium chloride — at cathode a colorless gas which is explosive when mixed with air; at anode a greenish yellow gas which has a chlorine odour and bleaches litmus; the solution becomes basic.

(iv) Water and Sulphuric acid — at cathode a colorless gas which is explosive when mixed with air; at anode a colorless gas which ignites a glowing splint.

Volume ratio $\dfrac{\text{gas at cathode}}{\text{gas at anode}} = \dfrac{2}{1}$

Conclusions — Ions produced in solution are attracted to the oppositely charged electrodes. The cations are the ions attracted to the cathode; the anions are the ions attracted to the anode. The movement of ions constitutes the current in the solution. A cation may be neutralized at the cathode by receiving one or more electrons from it. An anion may be neutralized at the anode by giving up one or more electrons to it.

(i) Hydrochloric acid —

$HCl \longrightarrow H^+ + Cl^-$

$H_2O \longrightarrow H^+ + OH^-$ (water ionizes slightly)

Cations are H^+

at cathode $2H^+ + 2$ electrons $\longrightarrow H_2 \uparrow$ (gas)

Anions are Cl^- and OH^- but Cl^- is much easier to neutralize so OH^- remains in solution.

at anode $2Cl^- \longrightarrow Cl_2 \uparrow + 2$ electrons

Hydrogen released at cathode and chlorine at anode.

(ii) Copper (II) Sulphate —

$CuSO_4 \longrightarrow Cu^{2+} + SO_4^{2-}$

$H_2O \longrightarrow H^+ + OH^-$

Cations Cu^{2+} and H^+ (Cu^{2+} easier to neutralize)

at cathode $Cu^{2+} + 2e \longrightarrow Cu$

Anions OH^- and SO_4^{2-} (OH^- easier to neutralize)

at anode $OH^- \longrightarrow OH + 1e$

$\qquad\qquad 4OH \longrightarrow 2H_2O + O_2 \uparrow$ (gas)

Copper released at cathode and oxygen at anode.

(iii) Sodium Chloride —

$NaCl \longrightarrow Na^+ + Cl^-$

$H_2O \longrightarrow H^+ + OH^-$

Cations Na^+ and H^+ (H^+ easier to neutralize)

at cathode $2H^+ + 2e \longrightarrow H_2 \uparrow$ (gas)

Anions Cl⁻ and OH⁻ (Cl⁻ easier to neutralize)

at anode $2Cl^- \longrightarrow Cl_2 \uparrow (gas) + 2e$

Hydrogen at cathode and chlorine at anode.

(iv) Water with hydrogen sulphate —

$H_2SO_4 \longrightarrow 2H^+ + SO_4^{2-}$

$H_2O \longrightarrow H^+ + OH^-$

Cations H^+

at cathode $2H^+ + 2e \longrightarrow H_2 \uparrow$

Anions OH^- and SO_4^{2-} (OH⁻ easier to neutralize)

at anode $OH^- \longrightarrow OH + 1e$

$\qquad\qquad 4OH \longrightarrow 2H_2O + O_2 \uparrow$

Hydrogen at cathode, oxygen at anode.

H_2SO_4 increases the conductivity but does not otherwise take part in the reaction.

An overall equation which includes reactions at both electrodes can be written for an electrolysis —

(a) $2HCl \longrightarrow H_2 \uparrow + Cl_2 \uparrow$

(b) $2CuSO_4 + 2H_2O \longrightarrow 2Cu + O_2 \uparrow + 2H_2SO_4$

(c) $2NaCl + 2H_2O \longrightarrow H_2 \uparrow + Cl_2 \uparrow + 2NaOH$

(d) $2H_2O \longrightarrow 2H_2 \uparrow + O_2 \uparrow$

4. ELECTRODE REACTIONS —

At the anode the reaction involves a transfer of electrons from ion to anode — this is an oxidation of the ion. At the cathode there is a transfer of electrons from cathode to ion — this is a reduction of the ion. It is evident from the experiment, in the previous section, that an ion oxidized or reduced may come from the solute or from the solvent.

5. ELECTRO CHEMICAL (ACTIVITY) SERIES —

This is a series of metals and hydrogen arranged in order of —

(i) decreasing activity (an atom is more active than another if it forms its ion more easily)

or (ii) increasing ease with which the ion accepts an electron(s) to become the atom.

This series includes the following (arranged in order as indicated above) — K, Ca, Na, Mg, Al, Zn, Fe, H, Pb, Cu, Hg, Ag.

6. OXIDATION AND REDUCTION –

In units VI and VII the reactions of metals with oxygen and dilute acids were described; these are electron transfers also and are therefore oxidations and reductions. Here oxidation and reduction occur in the same reaction which is called a redox reaction.

Oxidation = a loss of electrons

Reduction = a gain of electrons

If equations are written in ionic form the transfers of electrons are more obvious –

e.g. $2Mg + O_2 \longrightarrow 2Mg^{2+} + 2O^{2-}$ (i)

or $Mg + 2H^+ + 2Cl^- \longrightarrow Mg^{2+} + 2Cl^- + H_2$ (ii)

(or simply $Mg + 2H^+ \longrightarrow Mg^{2+} + H_2$)

In reaction (i) Mg loses 2 electrons to O; i.e. Mg is oxidized and O is reduced.

In reaction (ii) Mg loses 2 electrons to $2H^+$; i.e. Mg is oxidized and H^+ is reduced.

Metals above hydrogen in the electro chemical series will displace hydrogen from dilute acids – the rate of reaction is more rapid the nearer the metal is to the top of the series. The nearer the metal is to the top of the series the more readily it forms an oxide and the more stable is the oxide.

7. A COMMON ION may be responsible for similar properties of solutions of various compounds.

(a) Experiment – Colour produced by certain ions.

Method – Observe colours of dilute solutions of a number of salts of (i) copper (II) (ii) cobalt (II) and (iii) nickel (II).

Observations and Conclusions –

   (i)   Solutions are blue due to Cu^{2+} ion.

   (ii)   Solutions are pink due to Co^{2+} ion.

   (iii) Solutions are green due to Ni^{2+} ion.

(b) Experiment – Properties common to acids –

Method and observations – Test dilute solutions of HCl, H_2SO_4 and $HC_2H_3O_2$ as follows.

(i)   taste (very dilute)   — sour
(ii)   Litmus   — red
(iii) Bromthymol   — yellow
(iv) Baking soda solution   — colorless gas which turns lime-water milky.
(v)   Magnesium powder   — colorless gas which ignites.

Conclusions — All acids —
(i)   taste sour.
(ii)   turn litmus red.
(iii) turn bromthymol yellow.
(iv) react with $NaHCO_3$ to produce CO_2.
(v)   react with Mg to produce H_2.

These properties are due to the hydrogen ion (H^+) which is produced by all acids in solution.

An acid may be defined as a substance which produces hydrogen (hydronium) ion in solution.

(c) Experiment — Properties common to bases —
Method and observations — Test dilute solutions of NaOH, NH_4OH and $Ca(OH)_2$ as follows —

(i)   feel   — slippery
(ii)   litmus   — blue
(iii) bromthymol — blue
(iv) magnesium — no reaction.

Conclusions — All bases —
(i)   feel slippery
(ii)   turn litmus blue
(iii) turn bromthymol blue
(iv) do not react with Mg.

These are properties of the hydroxide ion (OH^-) which is released by all bases in solution.

A base may be defined as a substance which produces hydroxide ion in solution.

8. NEUTRALIZATION —

(a) When an acid and a base are mixed the hydrogen ion from the acid and the hydroxide ion from the base combine to form water; the ions of the salt produced remain in solution.

Experiment — To illustrate neutralization.
Method —
    (i)   to 10 ml. of a dilute solution of NaOH add a few drops of bromthymol solution.
    (ii) add a dilute solution of HCl slowly with dropper until solution turns green.
    (iii) evaporate solution to dryness and taste residue.

Observations —
White solid remains which tastes salty.

Conclusions —
Neutralization of an acid by a base produces water and a salt of the acid.

$$NaOH + HCl \longrightarrow H_2O + NaCl$$

The salt is in the form of ions (Na^+ and Cl^-) in solution. Other examples of neutralization are —

    (i) $Ca(OH)_2 + H_2SO_4 \longrightarrow 2H_2O + CaSO_4$

    (ii) $NH_4OH + HNO_3 \longrightarrow H_2O + NH_4NO_3$

  (b) Polyprotic acids — acids which contain more than one ionizable hydrogen atom — e.g. H_2SO_4, H_2CO_3 or H_3PO_4.
The hydrogen ions leave the molecule in steps —

e.g. $H_2SO_4 + H_2O \longrightarrow H_3O^+ + HSO_4^-$ (ionizes readily)

    $HSO_4^- + H_2O \longrightarrow H_3O^+ + SO_4^{2-}$ (ionizes slightly)

HSO_4^- is called the hydrogen sulphate ion.

  (c) Acid Salts — are salts in which fewer than the total number of ionizable hydrogen atoms have been replaced.

e.g. $NaHSO_4$, $NaHCO_3$, NaH_2PO_4 etc.

Naming — e.g. $NaHCO_3$ — sodium hydrogen carbonate is preferred rather than sodium bicarbonate.

        NaH_2PO_4 — sodium dihydrogen phosphate etc.

9. EXTENT OF CHEMICAL REACTIONS —

Reactions may or may not go to completion; certain factors which tend to make reactions go to completion (i.e. prevent reverse reactions from occurring) are indicated in (a), (b), (c), (d) below —

(a) Formation of an insoluble (or slightly soluble) salt —

Experiment — **Precipitation of an insoluble salt.**

Method — mix dilute solutions of —
  (i)   Lead (II) nitrate and potassium iodide
  (ii) Barium chloride and sodium sulphate
  (iii) Copper (II) chloride and sodium sulphide.

Observations —
  (i)   yellow precipitate (PbI_2)
  (ii) white precipitate $(BaSO_4)$
  (iii) black precipitate (CuS)

Conclusions — The reactants (salts) dissociate in solution and the salt which is insoluble precipitates.

  (i) $Pb^{2+} + 2NO_3^- + 2K^+ + 2I^- \longrightarrow PbI_2 \downarrow + 2K^+ + 2NO_3^-$

  or simply $Pb^{2+} + 2I^- \longrightarrow PbI_2 \downarrow$

This ionic equation represents the reaction better than the ordinary chemical equation —

$$Pb(NO_3)_2 + 2KI \longrightarrow PbI_2 + 2KNO_3$$

  (ii) $Ba^{2+} + 2Cl^- + 2Na^+ + SO_4^{2-} \longrightarrow BaSO_4 \downarrow + 2Na^+ + 2Cl^-$

  or simply $Ba^{2+} + SO_4^{2-} \longrightarrow BaSO_4 \downarrow$

  (iii) $Cu^{2+} + 2Cl^- + 2Na^+ + S^{2-} \longrightarrow CuS \downarrow + 2Na^+ + 2Cl^-$

  or simply $Cu^{2+} + S^{2-} \longrightarrow CuS \downarrow$

Solubility rules may be used to determine which, if any, compound will precipitate when solutions are mixed. Precipitation removes certain ions from the solution.

(b) Formation of a gas of low solubility —

Experiment — To illustrate formation of a gas.

Method —
   (i)   Add Mg metal to dilute HCl solution.
   (ii) Add Na_2CO_3 to dilute HCl.
  (iii) Add FeS to dilute HCl.

Observations —
   (i)   colorless gas evolved; gas burns.
   (ii) colorless gas which turns limewater milky
  (iii) colorless gas, unpleasant odour, (poisonous)

Conclusions —

   (i) $Mg + 2HCl \longrightarrow MgCl_2 + H_2 \uparrow$

   (ii) $Na_2CO_3 + 2HCl \longrightarrow 2NaCl + H_2O + CO_2 \uparrow$

  (iii) $FeS + 2HCl \longrightarrow FeCl_2 + H_2S \uparrow$

Hydrogen, carbon dioxide and hydrogen sulphide gases are only slightly soluble in water and therefore remove certain ions from the solution.

(c) Formation of an unionized (or slightly ionized) substance —
In the neutralization of an acid by a base, the ions H^+ and OH^- combine to form water which is only slightly ionized and therefore H^+ and OH^- are in effect removed from the solution.
The neutralization of any acid by any base can be written
   $H^+ + OH^- \longrightarrow H_2O$

(d) Position of metals in the electro chemical series —
If a metal is higher in the activity series it will displace another metal from a solution of its salt — this will go to completion.

Experiment — Displacement of metals by other metals.

Method —
   (i)   Add Zn to $Pb(NO_3)_2$ solution.
   (ii) Add Pb to $CuSO_4$ solution.
  (iii) Add Cu to $AgNO_3$ solution.
  (iv) Add Cu to $ZnSO_4$ solution.
  (v) Add Ag to $CuSO_4$ solution.

Observations —

(i) Black deposit on zinc.

(ii) Copper coloured deposit on lead; solution becomes colourless.

(iii) Silver crystals; solution becomes blue.

(iv) & (v) No change observed.

Conclusions —

(i) Zinc displaces lead $Zn + Pb^{2+} \longrightarrow Pb + Zn^{2+}$

(ii) Lead displaces copper $Pb + Cu^{2+} \longrightarrow Cu + Pb^{2+}$

(iii) Copper displaces silver $Cu + 2Ag^{+} \longrightarrow 2Ag + Cu^{2+}$

(iv) Copper does not displace zinc.

(v) Silver does not displace copper.

A metal higher in the electro chemical series displaces a metal lower; the reaction goes to completion because of difference in activity.

Experiment — **Relative positions of metals in the electrochemical series determined by reaction with dilute acid.**

Method — Add pieces of Mg, Zn, Fe, Cu, to dilute hydrochloric acid.

Observations — A colourless gas (hydrogen) is evolved with the first 3 metals but not with Cu. Rate of displacement of H_2 is greatest with Mg and least with Fe. Cu does not displace hydrogen.

Conclusion — the order of activity, (i.e. position in the electrochemical series), is Mg, Zn, Fe, H, Cu.

UNIT XII: THE ALKALINE EARTH ELEMENTS (GROUP 2)

I. MAGNESIUM AND CALCIUM are members of this group.

(a) Electron arrangements are similar (2, 8, 2 and 2, 8, 8, 2). Electrovalence of 2+ forming ions Mg^{2+} and Ca^{2+}. These are metals.

(b) Occurrence —
Magnesium — as carbonate in dolomite rock ($MgCO_3 \cdot CaCO_3$); as silicates (asbestos etc); in sea water (6 million tons per cubic mile) mainly $MgCl_2$.
Calcium — as carbonate (limestone, marble, chalk); in sea water (almost 2 million tons per cubic mile) mainly $CaCl_2$; gypsum rock ($CaSO_4 \cdot 2H_2O$).

(c) Production by electrolysis — These 2 metals are produced by electrolysis of the fused chlorides; the $MgCl_2$ is obtained from sea water or from magnesite ($MgCO_3$); the $CaCl_2$ is obtained as a by-product in the Solvay process for making Na_2CO_3. These chlorides, being ionic compounds, consist of mobile ions when fused — the cation Mg^{2+} or Ca^{2+} is reduced at the cathode.

Mg^{2+} + 2 electrons $\longrightarrow$ Mg (metal)
Ca^{2+} + 2 electrons $\longrightarrow$ Ca (metal)

(d) Physical properties — Both are soft silvery white metals of low density (1.75 g./ml. for Mg and 1.55 g./ml. for Ca). Melting points are $650°C$ for Mg and $850°C$ for Ca.

(e) Chemical properties —

Experiment — Chemical properties of Mg and Ca.

Method —
  (i)   Expose fresh surfaces of Mg & Ca to air.
  (ii) Ignite pieces of Mg and Ca.
  (iii) Add Ca to cold water; add Mg to cold and to hot water;

collect and test gas produced with burning splint; test solution with litmus.

(iv) Add small pieces of Mg and Ca to dilute HCl – test gas with splint.

Observations and Conclusions –

(i) Surfaces tarnish – Ca oxidizes to CaO; Mg forms in moist air a thin protective layer of MgO and $MgCO_3$.

(ii) Ca burns with a brick red flame – white solid produced –
$$2Ca + O_2 \longrightarrow 2CaO$$
Mg ribbon burns with a brilliant white flame – white solid produced – $2Mg + O_2 \longrightarrow 2MgO$.

(iii) Ca reacts rapidly; colourless gas formed which burns; litmus turns blue – $Ca + 2H_2O \longrightarrow Ca(OH)_2 + H_2 \uparrow$ white precipitate since $Ca(OH)_2$ is only slightly soluble. Mg reacts very slowly with cold water, slowly with hot water, colourless gas, white precipitate, litmus turns blue –
$$Mg + 2H_2O \longrightarrow Mg(OH)_2 + H_2 \uparrow$$
$Mg(OH)_2$ only slightly soluble in water.

(iv) Both react vigorously with dilute acid; colourless gas formed which burns.

$$Mg + 2HCl \longrightarrow MgCl_2 + H_2 \uparrow$$

$$Ca + 2HCl \longrightarrow CaCl_2 + H_2 \uparrow$$

(f) Oxides – MgO and CaO are stable white solids; very high melting points.

Formation –
MgO formed by (i) combustion of metal $2Mg + O_2 \longrightarrow 2MgO$
or (ii) heating the carbonate $MgCO_3 \longrightarrow MgO + CO_2$
CaO formed by (i) combustion of metal $2Ca + O_2 \longrightarrow 2CaO$
(ii) heating carbonate (limestone) in lime kiln –
$$CaCO_3 \longrightarrow CaO + CO_2.$$

Structure – The bonds in MgO and CaO are ionic – (e.g. Mg^{2+} O^{2-}). The structure of the solid in each case is a face – centered cubic lattice (6 oppositely charged ions surround each ion) – Fig. 31.

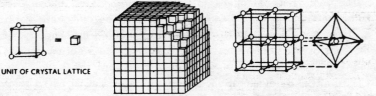

UNIT OF CRYSTAL LATTICE

Fig. 31 — A face — centered cubic crystal lattice.

Reaction of oxides with water — CaO (quickline) reacts with water releasing much heat —

$CaO + H_2O \longrightarrow Ca(OH)_2$ (slaked lime) — which is slightly soluble in water forming a basic solution (limewater).

MgO is slightly soluble in water forming a weakly basic solution $MgO + H_2O \longrightarrow Mg(OH)_2$.

Uses — CaO used for making glass, CaC_2 etc; largest use in making $Ca(OH)_2$ for mortar, plaster, softening water etc.

MgO — making refractory bricks for lining furnaces because of its very high melting point (2800^0C) and great stability.

Mixed with asbestos for steampipe insulation.

(g) Carbonates —

(i) **Natural occurrence** — $CaCO_3$ and $MgCO_3$ were mentioned above in 1 (b). When water with dissolved CO_2 is in contact with limestone or dolomite, some of the carbonate dissolves to form the hydrogen carbonate —

e.g. $CaCO_3 + H_2O + CO_2 \longrightarrow Ca(HCO_3)_2$

$Mg(HCO_3)_2$ is formed in the same way.

These hydrogen carbonates only exist as ions in solution (Ca^{2+} or Mg^{2+} and HCO_3^-); they cannot be obtained as pure substances since the hydrogen carbonate ion is unstable.

(ii) **Formation** — The oxide may combine with water to form the hydroxide which then may absorb CO_2 to form the carbonate; this reaction occurs in the setting of plaster or mortar (slaked lime, sand and water).

$CaO + H_2O \longrightarrow Ca(OH)_2$

$Ca(OH)_2 + CO_2 \longrightarrow CaCO_3 + H_2O$ (which evaporates)

i.e. mortar eventually becomes limestone and sand.

The hydrogen carbonate formation was outlined above. The hydrogen carbonate may decompose to form the carbonate — this happens for example in the formation of stalactites hanging from the roof of a limestone cave. Here a saturated solution containing Ca^{2+} and HCO_3^- drips through the roof of the cave, loses CO_2 and H_2O by evaporation, and precipitates $CaCO_3$ as an icicle hanging from the roof; this same reaction occurs in a tea kettle to form scale —

$$Ca(HCO_3)_2 \longrightarrow H_2O + CO_2 + CaCO_3 \downarrow$$

(iii) **Chemical properties** —

Experiment — Effect of heat and acids on Mg and Ca carbonates.

Method — Heat $MgCO_3$ powder in a test tube; pass gas into limewater; test residue with moist litmus.
Heat small pieces of $CaCO_3$ strongly in a crucible; test residue with moist litmus.
Add $MgCO_3$ and $CaCO_3$ separately to dilute HCl and dilute H_2SO_4; pass gas into limewater.

Observations and Conclusions —

Residue from $MgCO_3$ turns litmus blue; gas turns limewater milky - $MgCO_3$ decomposes readily on heating $MgCO_3 \longrightarrow MgO + CO_2$

Residue from heating $CaCO_3$ also turns litmus blue — higher temperature required to decompose $CaCO_3$

$$CaCO_3 \longrightarrow CaO + CO_2$$

Rapid effervescence of gas from either carbonate and a dilute strong acid — CO_2 produced

$$MgCO_3 + 2HCl \longrightarrow MgCl_2 + H_2O + CO_2 \uparrow$$

$$CaCO_3 + H_2SO_4 \longrightarrow CaSO_4 + H_2O + CO_2 \uparrow$$

(iv) **Uses** — $CaCO_3$ — building stone, crushed stone, source of quicklime (decomposes at $600^{\circ}C$).
$MgCO_3$ — source of MgO (decomposes by heat) source of Mg (Pidgeon process).

(h) **Hardness in Water** — is due to Ca^{2+} and Mg^{2+} which waste soap by reacting with it to form an insoluble sticky curd.

(i) Kinds of hardness and softening –

Temporary hardness is due to hydrogen carbonates of Mg and Ca; this can be softened by boiling which decomposes HCO_3^-.

$$Ca(HCO_3)_2 \longrightarrow CaCO_3 \downarrow + H_2O + CO_2 \text{ (same with Mg)}$$

This removes Ca^{2+} or Mg^{2+} from the water.

Permanent hardness is due to sulphates and chlorides of Mg and Ca. Here the metal ions cannot be removed by boiling but can be removed by certain chemicals such as washing soda (Na_2CO_3) etc.

e.g. $Na_2CO_3 + CaCl_2 \longrightarrow CaCO_3 \downarrow + 2NaCl$

Washing soda will also remove temporary hardness –

$Na_2CO_3 + Mg(HCO_3)_2 \longrightarrow 2NaHCO_3 + MgCO_3 \downarrow$

The ion exchange method of softening depends on the fact that certain organic resins, when in contact with water, will exchange the metal ions in the water for H^+ and the negative ions for OH^-; the H^+ and OH^- combine to form H_2O so that the product is comparable to distilled water.

(ii) Soaps and other detergents –

have similar cleaning actions. Dirt usually contains oily substances which are emulsified by detergents so that they can be washed away along with the solid dirt particles. Soap consists of soluble sodium salts of certain organic acids (stearic etc). In water containing Ca^{2+} and Mg^{2+} ions, the soap reacts to form insoluble Ca and Mg salts of these acids, which precipitate as grey sticky curd (bath-tub ring): the soap cannot have any detergent action until all the Ca^{2+} and Mg^{2+} ions are precipitated. Synthetic detergents produce no precipitate with hard water and some have low – foaming characteristics which are desirable for some purposes.

Experiment – Hardness in Water

Method – Prepare temporary hard water by passing CO_2 through 100 ml. of limewater until it clears – this is sample A. Prepare permanent hard water by adding a few grains of $CaCl_2$ (or $MgSO_4$) to 100 ml. of distilled water – sample B. Using 10 ml.

portions of A and B and distilled (soft) water, do the soap test (find number of drops of soap solution needed to give a good lather on shaking). Using the same soap test find the effects on A and B of boiling and of adding a pinch of Na_2CO_3.

Conclusions — Amount of soap needed is a test for hardness. Observations and explanations were covered in h (i).

(i) Sulphates — Magnesium sulphate ($MgSO_4$) is found in water of many mineral springs — when evaporated epsom salt ($MgSO_4 \cdot 7H_2O$) crystallizes.

Gypsum ($CaSO_4 \cdot 2H_2O$), a white crystalline solid occurs naturally; this is slightly soluble in water causing hardness. Heated to 140^0C gypsum loses part of its water of hydration, forming Plaster of Paris.

$$2CaSO_4 \cdot 2H_2O \longrightarrow (CaSO_4)_2 \cdot H_2O + 3H_2O$$

Plaster of Paris is a white powder which reacts rapidly with water at room temperature to revert to gypsum (the reverse of the above reaction). Slight expansion during this setting process makes it useful in taking casts.

2. THE ALKALINE EARTH ELEMENTS are beryllium, magnesium calcium, strontium, barium, radium. These metals all have 2 electrons in the outer shell and can give them up to form the ion M^{2+} with the electron configuration of an inert gas.

These elements all have the following characteristics —

    (i)   electropositive (form positive ions)

    (ii) hydroxides sparingly soluble in water and are fairly weak bases.

    (iii) carbonates decompose on heating (CO_2 given off)

    (iv) hydrogen carbonates exist only in solution.

3. Gradations in reactivities are shown by the alkaline earth elements. In the following table the electron arrangements, atomic radii and ionization energies are compared.

SYMBOL	ATOMIC NUMBER	ELECTRON SHELLS K ⟶ Q	ATOMIC RADIUS IN ANGSTROMS 1 ANGSTROM = 10⁻⁸ CM.	IONIZATION ENERGY IN KCAL. PER MOLE 1ST. ELECTRON	2ND. ELECTRON
Be	4	2, 2	1.11	214	420
Mg	12	2, 8, 2	1.60	175	345
Ca	20	2, 8, 8, 2	1.97	140	275
Sr	38	2, 8, 18, 8, 2	2.15	132	253
Ba	56	2, 8, 18, 18, 8, 2	2.17	120	230
Ra	88	2, 8, 18, 32, 18, 8, 2			

Going down this group from Be to Ba the following gradations in properties can be shown —

   (i)   metals are more reactive
   (ii) hydroxides are stronger bases
   (iii) carbonates are more stable
   (iv) ionization energies are smaller.

Ionization energy is the energy required to remove the most loosely held electron — this is sometimes called ionization potential and given in electron — volts (1 electron — volt = 23 Kcal. per mole).

The above gradations are related to the following structural features of these atoms —

As atomic number increases —

   (i)   atoms become larger
   (ii) valence electrons are farther from the nuclius
   (iii) the inner electron shells have a shielding effect
   (iv) valence electrons are held less tightly
   (v) the atoms become more active.

UNIT XIII: THE HALOGEN ELEMENTS (GROUP 7)

Fluorine (F), Chlorine (Cl), Bromine (Br), Iodine (I), Astatine (At).

I. THE HALIDES — The halogens all have 7 electrons in the outer shell and therefore readily accept one electron to form a stable octet; this produces the halide ions F^-, Cl^-, Br^- and I^- (little work has been done with astatine). The halogens are non-metals. The halides are compounds of these halide ions with metals or hydrogen — e.g. HBr, KI, NaF, AgCl etc.

(a) Occurrence — Chloride ion and bromide ion occur in sea water and as halides of Na, Mg, K and Ca in salt beds. Fluoride ion in small amounts in some natural waters. Iodide ion in small amounts in sea water — concentrated in sea weeds. Insoluble halides occur as mineral deposits — e.g. CaF_2 (fluorspar) in United states, England etc.; AgBr in South America and Mexico; $HgBr_2$ in Mexico.

(b) Properties of Na and K halides — These are all white crystalline solids which form cubic crystals; a single crystal is colorless and transparent; all are soluble in water.

(c) Silver halides —

Experiment — **Properties of silver halides**

Method —
(i)   Place 10 ml. of dilute solutions of NaCl, NaBr, and NaI in separate test tubes.
(ii) To each add a few drops of dilute $AgNO_3$ solution.
(iii) Add some aqueous ammonia to each.
(iv) Repeat (i) and (ii) and leave exposed to sunlight.

Observations —
In (ii) a curdy precipitate is formed in each case, white with NaCl, cream coloured with NaBr and yellow with NaI.

89

In (iii) the AgCl dissolves, the AgBr partially dissolves and the AgI is insoluble.

In (iv) all 3 silver halides darken on exposure to light; AgCl becomes violet then black.

Conclusions —

$$AgNO_3 + NaCl \longrightarrow AgCl \downarrow + NaNO_3$$
$$AgNO_3 + NaBr \longrightarrow AgBr \downarrow + NaNO_3$$
$$AgNO_3 + NaI \longrightarrow AgI \downarrow + NaNO_3$$

or $Ag^+ + X^- \longrightarrow AgX \downarrow$ (X^- is the halide ion)

All 3 silver halides are insoluble in water — they show gradation in solubility in NH_4OH solution.

(Silver Fluoride (AgF) is a yellow solid soluble in water).

The formation of AgBr and AgI show the formation of coloured compounds from colourless ions.

Silver halides are decomposed by light forming silver metal.

(d) Hydrogen halides —

Experiments — Preparation of HCl.

Method — Warm NaCl with concentrated H_2SO_4 as in Fig. 32. Blow breath over bottle of gas. Test solution with litmus and with zinc metal.

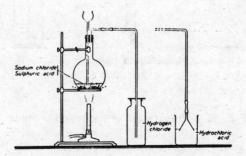

Fig. 32. Preparation of Hydrogen Chloride

Observations — A colourless gas with a sharp irritating odour is produced; gas dissolves readily — solution turns litmus red and reacts with zinc producing hydrogen; gas fumes in moist air (breath).

Conclusions —

$$NaCl + H_2SO_4 \longrightarrow NaHSO_4 + HCl \uparrow$$

HCl is very soluble in water (500 litres per litre of water at S.T.P.) forming a strong acid (hydrochloric) for which we use the same formula. Fog (fumes) is produced because the soluble gas condenses water vapour from the air to produce droplets of dilute hydrochloric acid.

Experiment — Properties of HBr and HI.

Method — Because of their instability these compounds cannot be made by the same method as HCl (see next experiment). These gases are made by the reaction of Bromine or Iodine with red phosphorus and water as illustrated in Fig. 33.

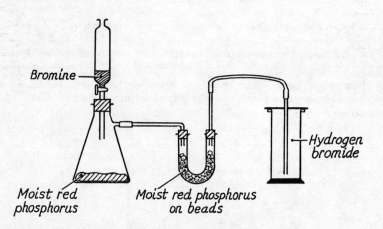

Fig. 33 — Preparation of Hydrogen bromide.

Dissolve gases in water and test solutions with litmus; blow breath over gas.

Observations – HBr and HI are colourless gases, sharp irritating odour, very soluble in water, strongly acidic solution, fumes in moist air.

Conclusions – The reaction, in each case, is hydrolysis of the bromide or iodide –

$$3Br_2 + 2P \longrightarrow 2PBr_3$$

$$PBr_3 + 3H_2O \longrightarrow H_3PO_3 + 3HBr$$

A similar reaction occurs with iodine. The U tube in Fig. 33 is to remove any Br_2 or I_2 vapour.

The acids formed by dissolving in water are hydrobromic (HBr) and Hydriodic (HI).

Chlorides, bromides, and iodides are salts of the 3 acids – hydrochloric, hydrobromic and hydriodic.

HF is described in 2 (b).

Experiments – **Stability of hydrogen halides** –

Method –
(i) To 1 cm. of NaCl in a test tube add a few drops of concentrated H_2SO_4; warm gently; note colour, odour etc. of gas.
(ii) Repeat (i) with NaBr
(iii) Repeat (i) with NaI.

Observations –
(i) colourless gas; sharp irritating odour; fumes strongly in moist air.
(ii) red-brown gas; choking odour; odour of SO_2 detected; some fuming.
(iii) violet vapour; no fuming; choking odour, odour of H_2S detected; steel grey crystals on sides of test tube.

Conclusions –
(i) $NaCl + H_2SO_4 \longrightarrow NaHSO_4 + HCl \uparrow$
HCl is a stable compound and, when produced, is released without further reaction.
(ii) Some of the HBr produced is oxidized by H_2SO_4 to produced Br_2 and SO_2 which are released along with HBr.
$$NaBr + H_2SO_4 \longrightarrow NaHSO_4 + HBr$$
$$2HBr + H_2SO_4 \longrightarrow SO_2 + Br_2 + 2H_2O$$

(iii) Most of the HI produced is oxidized by H_2SO_4 to produce I_2 and H_2S.

$$NaI + H_2SO_4 \longrightarrow NaHSO_4 + HI$$
$$8HI + H_2SO_4 \longrightarrow H_2S + 4I_2 + 4H_2O$$

HCl is stable. HBr is less stable and is partially oxidized by H_2SO_4. HI is least stable and is readily oxidized by H_2SO_4.

HBr and HI are reducing agents.

2. THE HALOGENS —

In the laboratory these elements are prepared by the oxidation of the halide ion by manganese dioxide and concentrated sulphuric acid. They are all irritating to the skin and poisonous if inhaled as gases.

(a) Experiment — Preparation and properties of chlorine —

Method — Fig. 34.

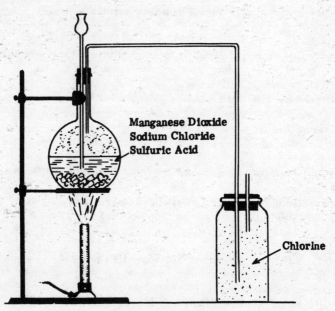

Manganese Dioxide
Sodium Chloride
Sulfuric Acid

Chlorine

Fig. 34 — Preparation of Chlorine

(i)   Note state, colour, odour of chlorine.
(ii) Expose moist red and blue litmus to chlorine.
(iii) Add 1 inch of water to a test tube of Cl_2 and shake, then add 1 ml. of CCl_4 to same test tube — shake and let settle.
(iv) Lower a piece of hot Cu foil into a bottle of Cl_2.
(v)   Lower a piece of white P in a **deflagrating** spoon into a bottle of Cl_2.

Observations —
(i)   greenish yellow gas with a choking odour.
(ii) blue litmus turns red then bleaches.
(iii) pale greenish yellow solution; colour leaves H_2O solution and CCl_4 settles as a yellow solution.
(iv) Cu glows and forms a greenish yellow solid coating.
(v)   yellow flame; white fumes.

Conclusions —
$$2NaCl + MnO_2 + 3H_2SO_4 \longrightarrow Cl_2 \uparrow + 2NaHSO_4 + MnSO_4 + 2H_2O$$
Chlorine solution in water is acidic and is a bleaching agent. Chlorine is moderately soluble in water (2 volumes Cl_2 to 1 volume H_2O at room temperature). Chlorine is more soluble in CCl_4 than in H_2O.
Copper (a metal) reacts with chlorine —
$$Cu + Cl_2 \longrightarrow CuCl_2 \quad \text{(copper (II) chloride)}$$
Phosphorus (a non-metal) also reacts with chlorine —
$$2P + 3Cl_2 \longrightarrow 2PCl_3 \quad \text{both chlorides}$$
$$\text{or } 2P + 5Cl_2 \longrightarrow 2PCl_5 \quad \text{are formed.}$$

(b) Experiment — Chlorine solution in water —

Method —
(i)   Pass Cl_2 through water until the solution is distinctly coloured (greenish-yellow).
(ii) Place various coloured materials in the Cl_2 solution.
(iii) Let stand in sunlight for several days — Fig. 35.
(iv) Test gas collected, with a glowing splint.
(v)   Test solution with litmus.

94

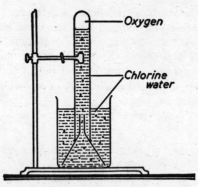

Fig. 35 – Chlorine solution in sunlight.

Observations –
(ii) many coloured substances are bleached.
(iii) & (iv) colourless gas collected ignites a glowing splint.
(v) solution remaining is acidic.

Conclusions –
Some of the dissolved chlorine reacts with water –
$$H_2O + Cl_2 \longrightarrow HCl + HClO \quad \text{(hypochlorous acid)}$$
Both dissolved chlorine and hypochlorous acid are oxidizing agents which bleach by oxidizing pigments.
The HClO on standing decomposes –
$$2HClO \longrightarrow 2HCl + O_2 \uparrow$$
The remaining solution contains HCl and is therefore acidic.

(c) Experiment – Preparation and Properties of Bromine –

Method – Fig. 36.

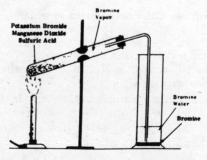

Fig. 36 – Preparation of Bromine

(i)　Observe state, colour, etc. of bromine.

(ii)　Collect several bottles of bromine vapour.

(iii)　Expose moist litmus to bromine vapour.

(iv)　Add 1 ml. of CCl_4 to 10 ml. of Br_2 solution in water; shake and let settle.

(v)　Heat Cu foil and lower into Br_2 vapour.

(vi)　Lower white P into Br_2 vapour.

(vii)　Place coloured materials in Br_2 solution.

Observations —

(i) Bromine at room temperature is a dark red liquid, more dense than water; it readily forms a reddish brown vapour (boiling point is 59^0C); Br_2 is quite soluble in H_2O forming a reddish brown solution. CCl_4 takes colour from water solution and forms a brown solution. Litmus turns red than bleaches; some materials bleach. Black deposit forms on copper. Phosphorus forms a yellow solid.

Conclusions —

$$2NaBr + MnO_2 + 3H_2SO_4 \longrightarrow Br_2 + 2NaHSO_4 + MnSO_4 + 2H_2O$$

Br_2 is an oxidizing and bleaching agent but not as active as chlorine.

Br_2 is quite soluble in H_2O but more soluble in CCl_4.

Br_2 reacts with metals and non-metals but not as actively as does chlorine —

$$Cu + Br_2 \longrightarrow CuBr_2$$
$$2P + 5Br_2 \longrightarrow 2PBr_5 \quad \text{(or } PBr_3\text{)}$$

(d) Experiment — Preparation and Properties of Iodine.

Method — Fig. 37.

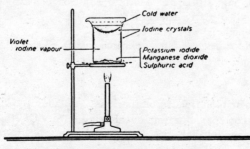

Fig. 37 — Preparation of Iodine

(i)   Observe deposit on underside of evaporating dish.

(ii)   Add iodine crystals to 10 ml. of water in test tube and shake.

(iii) Add 1 ml. of CCl_4 to solution in (ii) — shake and let settle.

(iv)   Warm I_2 crystals in test tube and expose to moist litmus.

(v)   Into vapour produced in (iv) lower a piece of hot Cu foil.

(vi)   Into I_2 vapour lower some white phosphorus.

Observations —

(i)   Purplish black crystals (I_2) form on evaporating dish.

(ii)   Pale brownish solution forms.

(iii) Brown colour of water solution disappears; CCl_4 settles as a violet solution.

(iv)   Iodine forms a violet vapour on warming — no bleaching effect on litmus.

(v)   Cu becomes coated with a white solid.

(vi)   P forms a dark red solid.

Conclusions —

$$2NaI + MnO_2 + 3H_2SO_4 \longrightarrow I_2 + 2NaHSO_4 + 8H_2O + 2MnSO_4$$

I_2 sublimes readily; I_2 is slightly soluble in H_2O — more soluble in CCl_4; I_2 combines with metals and non-metals but less actively than Cl_2 or Br_2.

$$2Cu + I_2 \longrightarrow 2CuI$$

$$2P + 3I_2 \longrightarrow 2PI_3$$

(e) Experiment — Displacement of halogens —

Method —

(i)   Through 10 ml. of a dilute solution of NaBr bubble Cl_2; then add 3 ml. of CCl_4, shake and let settle.

(ii)   Repeat (i) with NaI solution.

(iii) Add 5 ml. of Br_2 solution to 10 ml. of NaI solution; then add 3 ml. of CCl_4, shake and let settle.

Observations —

(i)   NaBr solution is colourless; on adding Cl_2 the NaBr solution becomes red-brown; on shaking with CCl_4 the red-brown colour disappears and the CCl_4 settles as a brown solution.

(ii) NaI solution is colourless; turns brown on adding Cl_2; loses its colour on shaking with CCl_4 which settles as a violet solution.

Conclusions —

Chlorine displaces Br_2 or I_2 from solutions containing Br^- or I^- ions.

Bromine displaces I_2 from solutions containing I^- ion.

$$Cl_2 + 2Br^- \longrightarrow Br_2 + 2Cl^-$$

$$Cl_2 + 2I^- \longrightarrow I_2 + 2Cl^-$$

$$Br_2 + 2I^- \longrightarrow I_2 + 2Br^-$$

Relative activity is shown by these displacement reactions. Chlorine is the most active of these 3 halogens, bromine next and iodine least.

(f) Fluorine and its compounds —

(i) Fluorine is a pale yellow gas — the most active of the halogens; it combines with all elements at room temperature (except N and O).

(ii) Sodium fluoride (NaF) is a white crystalline solid; an insecticide; an anti-fungus in wood treatment; added to water supply to prevent tooth decay.

(iii) Hydrogen fluoride (H_2F_2) — a colourless liquid. (B.P. 19.5^0C); volatile, poisonous, corrosive; a weak acid in solution; used in etching glass, making freons, making cryolite for electrolytic extraction of Al, as a catalyst in gasoline production.

(g) Astatine — very radioactive; first prepared in 1940; least active of the halogens.

3. COMPARISON OF PROPERTIES OF THE HALOGENS —

All of the halogens have 7 valence electrons and in chemical reactions tend to gain 1 electron to have a stable outer shell of 8 electrons, thereby forming the halide ion (1^-). The 7 valence electrons are evidently held tightly by all of the halogens since the ionization energies are large (see the following table); atoms of these elements therefore tend to attract electrons from other atoms and have an oxidizing effect. The halogens form di-atomic molecules by sharing a pair of electrons (Cl_2 etc).

SYMBOL	ATOMIC NUMBER	ELECTRON CONFIGURATION K ⟶ O	IONIC RADIUS (1⁻ ION) ANGSTROMS	IONIZATION ENERGY (KCAL./MOLE)
F	9	2, 7	1.36	401.5
Cl	17	2, 8, 7	1.81	300
Br	35	2, 8, 18, 7	1.95	273
I	53	2, 8, 18, 18, 7	2.16	241

The activity of an atom depends on —

(i) distance from the + charged nucleus to the valence electrons.

(ii) size of the + charge on the nucleus.

(iii) shielding effect of the electron shels between the nucleus and the valence electrons.

From the above table it is evident that as the atomic number (and molecular weight) increases, the distance from nucleus to valence electrons and the shielding effect increase; these tend to decrease attraction for valence electrons; the increased attraction due to increased nuclear charge apparently has less effect as shown by the decrease in ionization energy. The fluorine atom therefore has the greatest attraction for electrons — i.e. it is the most active (the greatest oxidizing action).

Experiments, described above, indicated that activity decreased in the order Cl_2, Br_2, I_2.

Physical properties of the halogens also show gradation with atomic number.

SYMBOL	STATE (ROOM TEMP.)	COLOUR	MELTING POINT (⁰C)	BOILING POINT (⁰C)
F	Gas	light yellow	−223	−187
Cl	Gas	greenish yellow	−102	−35
Br	Liquid	reddish brown	−7	+59
I	Solid	violet	+114	+183

The hydrogen halides were studied in Unit XIII 1; they are similar in that they are colourless gases, very soluble in water forming strongly acidic solutions (except H_2F_2); they show gradation in stability from quite stable HCl to less stable HBr to unstable HI.

UNIT XIV: THE PERIODIC CLASSIFICATION

Early attempts at classification of elements were made by Dobereiner (1817), Newlands (1863), Mendeléeff (1869), Meyer (1871) etc. The modern form of the Periodic Table is a modified version of Mendeléeff's table which was based on observations that there was a periodic recurrence of properties if the elements were arranged in order of increasing atomic weight. In the modern table the elements are arranged in order of increasing atomic number, a recurrence of chemical properties occurring at intervals of 2, 8, 8, 18, 18, and 32 elements; a new horizontal row is started at each of these intervals so that elements of similar properties form vertical rows; a horizontal row is a period; a vertical row is a group.

In Unit II the relation of electron arrangement to atomic number was indicated; from this it is evident that, in a group, the elements have the same number of valence electrons, and that, going from left to right in a period, the valence ring of the series of elements is gradually filled to the maximum of eight.

Fig. 38 shows relative sizes of atoms in a simplified periodic table.

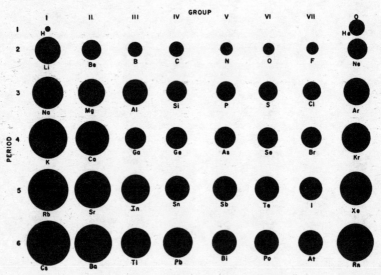

Fig. 38. — Relative sizes of atoms.

Elements in Groups 1 and 2 are active metals. Groups 6 and 7 include the active non-metals. Group 0 is made up of the inert gases (stable octet in outer shell).

Elements in a group, since they have the same number of valence electrons, have the same valence and similar chemical properties.

In Unit XII 3 the reasons for increase in metallic activity with increase in atomic number in Group 2 were discussed. In Unit XIII 3 the decrease in non-metallic activity with increase in atomic number in Group 7 was discussed.

Going from left to right in a Period (e.g. Period 3), the atomic radius decreases as the positive nuclear charge and electron number increase; therefore there is an increasing tendency to attract electrons and a corresponding rise in ionization energy from Na to Cl; there is therefore a gradation from metallic Na to non-metallic Cl.

NOTES

NOTES

NOTES

NOTES

NOTES

NOTES

NOTES